A RANGER PURE AND SIMPLE

The Evolution of Parks and Park Rangers in America

THOMAS A. SMITH

Foreword by James Brady
Former Chief Ranger, National Park Service

A Ranger Pure and Simple

ISBN: 978-1-61170-202-6

Correspondence may be sent to the author via email: ilvparks@verizon.net

Cover courtesy of Thomas Habecker.

Second Edition 2016.

Printed in the USA and UK on acid-free paper.

Robertson Publishing™
www.RobertsonPublishing.com

To purchase additional copies of this book go to:
amazon.com
barnesandnoble.com

Also by Thomas Smith:

I'm Just a Seasonal: The Life of a Seasonal Ranger in Yosemite National Park.

Dedicated to Mildred,
my companion for almost 60 years
and to my brother Bob,
whom the Lord took in April, 2013.

Table of Contents

Acknowledgements

The author would like to thank the following people:

Paul Romero, former Chief Deputy Director, California State Parks and former Director of Santa Clara County Department of Parks and Recreation. Several years ago, Paul and I had a discussion about writing this book, and he was very supportive during the process. A most learned park professional, Paul gave some great background material.

Thomas Habecker NPS (ret.), my Tuolumne Meadows Supervisor, retired as a Denali (Alaska) District Ranger. Tom contributed several pictures to this book and also contributed editorial comments.

Harry Batlin, California State Park Regional Director (ret.), reviewed the book for State Park content. Harry is one of the most knowledgeable park people I know and is a good friend.

Raleigh Young, Santa Clara County Parks and Recreation (ret.), helped me with my county ranger history and did research for me about some of the early enforcement problems in the county.

Jeff Price, California State Parks (ret.), sent my first survey out to the Gray Bears, a retired State Park group and offered editorial comments on content.

Jeff Ohlfs, Chief Ranger at Joshua Tree National Park, is a former student of mine. An amateur park historian, he read the drafts and helped with some of the historic material in this book.

James Brady, former Chief Ranger for the National Park Service and retired NPS Superintendent, reviewed the content and we had many long telephone conversations about where the ranger profession is going. Jim is a winner of the Lifetime Harry Yount Award, which is given to a person in the National Park Service who exemplifies what a ranger ought to be: the Ranger's Ranger. He wrote the foreword to this book. While Jim was elk hunting in Colorado in October of 2013, he sustained broken bones and serious head injuries in an accident riding an ATV. A draft of the foreword was found on his desk and finished, with his approval, by the author. Jim is now recovering at home in Durango.

Douglas Morris, National Park Service (ret.), former Superintendent at Shenandoah National Park, Albright Training Center Instructor, is now a consultant to parks all over the world. Doug read an earlier draft and sent me a position paper that he had written about the changing culture of the park ranger. I often used Doug, a great teacher, in our in-service training at West Valley College.

Don Rocha, Santa Clara County Natural Resource Manager. Don is also a former student. He shared his knowledge, his pictures, and his expertise on resource management and Office 2010.

Pam Helmke, another former student and a Senior Ranger for the City of San Jose Parks, did a lot of research on Saint James Park and Frederick Olmsted's possible involvement in that park's design.

Although academia does not seem to like Wikipedia, I found that the site had accurate information and I used it often.

I would also like to thank the following rangers who gave me their opinions about the role of the ranger in modern times:

> Bruce McKeeman, National Park Service (ret.)
> John Tucker, National Park Service (ret.)
> Bob Pavik, California State Parks (ret.)
> Miles Standish, Castle Rock State Park, California State Parks (ret.)
> Bill Krumbein, California State Parks (ret.)
> Dana Long, California State Parks (ret.)
> Charles "Butch" Farabee (ret.), National Park Service and a successful author of several books on parks and the duties of the ranger.

Thanks to:

Lee Shackleton, National Park Service (now deceased), was Chief Law Enforcement Investigator for Yosemite when I worked there.

Dave Carle, California State Parks (ret.). Dave and his wife Janet shared a full time position protecting and educating people about Mono Lake on California's East side.

Bob Binnewese, National Park Service and former Superintendent of Yosemite (ret.).

Roger Dittberner, Former Lieutenant, Tuolumne County Sheriff Department (ret.), who started his enforcement career as a seasonal ranger in Yosemite.

Jack Fry, National Park Service Seasonal Ranger for 26 seasons, (ret.). When Jack Fry left the naturalists to join the protection division in Yosemite, Will Neeley, a Yosemite naturalist icon, said to him, "Jack, you are now going to become a ranger, pure and simple." Thanks to Jack and Will, that became the title of this book.

Fred Koegler spent almost 50 seasons in Tuolumne Meadows in Yosemite. After being a protection ranger for many years, he patrolled the Hetch Hetchy watershed on a horse. He and his wife Debbie have visited every national park in the system.

Dana Long, California State Parks (ret.) sent me a lot of state park info.

James Sano, a long-time family friend and a former Yosemite naturalist who is an ecotourism expert, provided me marketing suggestions.

Chris Cruz, Park Management Instructor, West Valley College, Seasonal Ranger in Lassen National Park, and a former permanent ranger in the National Park Service.

I would also like to thank all those who participated in my survey at the California Training Conference in Seaside, California, in March 2013.

My son David Smith, a high school history teacher, contributed his expertise to the section on the United States Cavalry in Yosemite, which was a part of his Master's Thesis at San Jose State University.

My son R. Robert (Bob) Smith proofread the document. Bob, a supervisor with California Fish and Wildlife, is an accomplished article writer.

Another son, Dr. James Smith, an atmospheric researcher and a computer whiz, bailed me out of several computer software issues. I could not have written anything without his expertise because he built my computer! He also helped with the formatting of this document.

I cannot even tell you how much help and expertise I had from Kay Whipple. Kay edited the document for me and came up with some answers to my flow problems.

A last tribute goes to Bill Supernaugh, NPS (ret.), who reviewed my first book in the *Ranger Journal* of the Association of National Park Rangers. He passed away in November 2006. Bill once told me in an email correspondence that what he would really like to see is for rangers to truly "range" again.

Foreword

Preserving and setting aside "special places" called parks is a uniquely American idea that has been exported to over 120 nations worldwide. Viewed collectively, national, state, county, and regional park units throughout the United States combine to preserve and protect our nation's natural majesties, ecological integrity, and cultural heritage. Tom's historical analysis clearly shows that "parks are parks," regardless of location and size. Whether Santa Clara County California's regional parks or Yosemite National Park, all park units or protected areas share a common management philosophy: to preserve, protect, and provide opportunities for public use and enjoyment.

Besides recreation, adventure, natural beauty, and solitude, parks serve as outdoor learning laboratories, where one can explore and learn about the natural and cultural resources that are integral to every park unit. As such, American and international park visitors have a high appreciation of park values and an expectation that they will be well managed and protected for current and future generations. To meet this goal requires an informed and educated public that this book will help provide.

Parks are an American legacy. The visiting public also shares a fascination, if not a curiosity, about the rangers who work and perhaps live in the parks.

In his second book on parks, Thomas A. Smith (aka "Smitty") draws on his life experiences as a park management professor, coach, author, park management consultant, and longtime park ranger to give us a highly informative, carefully researched, and very readable insight into the collective origins, history, and evolution of parks and park rangers in America.

Moreover, what distinguishes this book from others on the origins of the United States park movement is that Smitty also provides a very personalized and often (behind the scenes) historical and contemporary analysis of the operational challenges for all park units and rangers nationwide.

He explains that second only to shrinking budgets/staffing considerations, a major ranger operational concern and decision point for parks in all jurisdictions is whether the protection rangers must be "specialists" in law enforcement or can also be a combination of what has been known and well established for a hundred years or so, as the "generalist ranger." That would be a ranger who is equally skilled and trained in fire prevention and suppression, emergency medical, safety, search and rescue, wildlife and backcountry operations, resource education/interpretation, and related visitor services as well as law enforcement responsibilities.

Historically, the generalist ranger has been defined as a "ranger for all reasons and seasons, a true protector, educator, and ambassador." However, as we know, both in fact and reality, "the times they are a changing." Much like the rest of society, organizations, and cultures, how park organizations deal with that change is the key issue.

Smitty identifies how an ever-expanding knowledge base including: "lessons learned," technological advances in communications, resource understandings, fire operations, search and rescue, medical and law enforcement/protection techniques, along with evolving standards of care and subsequent public expectations, has resulted in ranger specialists in all fields of park management. Specialists are now commonly found in resource management, interpretation, fire operations, and law enforcement. He acknowledges that this has been a necessary and needed change toward meeting the professional responsibilities of resource and visitor protection for ranger operations in parks nationwide.

But as he points out very clearly and asks the question "must this be at the expense of the park ranger generalist?" Clearly, both are needed. However, as the park ranger generalist is indeed a "multi-skilled specialist," the position is very, very cost effective, especially with restricted and diminishing park operational budgets and subsequent staffing levels. This is particularly true in smaller or medium-sized park operations that constitute most of the park agencies and units in this country.

Smitty further identifies and discusses both the complex attitudinal and skill responsibilities of law enforcement rangers. In all jurisdictions, law enforcement rangers must be highly trained to be effective, and they must also be trained in natural and cultural resources protection as well as visitor protection. In order to achieve the preventive goals of law enforcement (opportunity to know in advance what behavior is expected) they must be resource educators as well. This skill entails developing an operational knowledge of their park resources and having excellent interpretive and related communication skills.

A key atavistic consideration is what from the past should be brought forward that has value relative to very successful park ranger operations over the past 100 years?" As former ranger and national park superintendent, Jack Morehead described in the foreword of Smitty's first book, *I'm Just a Seasonal*, "rangers make important, often life-threatening decisions in stressful and emotional situations with no one else to confer with or assist. Their actions represent their entire organization, and establish a reputation for excellence. A positive public service attitude and the self-sufficiency and ability to operate independently are critical and as valuable today as in the past."

Smitty suggests, and I most whole-heartedly concur, that most important in being a truly professional park ranger (generalist or specialist) would be exercising an attitude of diversified public service in their daily operations. Yes, I can do that, yes I know what that flower is, and yes I can help you here and now!

The reader, particularly park professionals and related interested parties, will benefit from Smitty's analysis and discussion on these very substantive issues.

Note: Jim Brady retired after 38 years in the National Park Service, as Superintendent of Glacier Bay NP in Alaska in 1998. Highlights of his career include:

Seasonal Ranger; Crater Lake & Yellowstone 1961-1962

Park Ranger Petrified Forest National Park and Lake Mead National Recreation Area 1962-1967

Valley District Ranger, Yosemite 1972-1976

Instructor/Director of the Albright Training Center 1976-1981

Regional Chief Ranger, North Atlantic Region 1981-1983

Deputy Superintendent, Zion and Grand Teton 1983-1989

National Chief Ranger, Washington, DC 1991-1995

Developed training/management programs for national parks in Canada, Australia, Egypt and Turkey

Trained 1,000 employees in the Texas State Park System.

Introduction

I was walking with a ranger one day in a park parking lot and we noticed a potato chip bag lying on the ground. "Aren't you going to pick that up," I asked. "Nah, the ranger said, not my job and I'm tired of picking up after people." Taken aback by the rebuff, I reached over and picked it up myself. Although I resist putting all rangers into that barrel, I began to wonder. Is that where we really are in this profession? Are there more people out there working in parks with that kind of attitude? Do we really have people who seem to have no "land ethic" working in parks? Land ethic to me means a personal involvement with the outdoors, and a passion and a deep fondness for what nature contributes to the quality of life. It also means a commitment to land stewardship and an obligation to make sure that future generations have parks and outdoor spaces to enjoy.

Later, while visiting Yosemite, a ranger in Tuolumne Meadows told me that some of the new people did not even want to be called park rangers! They would rather be called "Federal Park Law Enforcement Officers," and they were not particularly interested in managing resources, giving interpretive talks, or anything other than writing tickets and making arrests.

An outdoor writer from a San Francisco Bay Area newspaper recently wrote in a March 2013 Sunday edition about a contact he had had with a California State Park Ranger in the parking lot of a local state park. The writer was trying to put a leash on his dog. The newspaper column, with the headline "Ranger's Bad Attitude" told about the ranger who gave the writer a bad time and appeared to be frustrated over not being able to cite the writer for anything. The interaction was bad enough for the writer to put it in the newspaper. Of course, I would think that even rangers sometimes get up on the wrong side of the bed.

A couple of years ago, a local county ranger I was with could not identify a bay tree in his park. It was a park full of bay trees. The excuse he gave was that he had only worked in that park for two years! An over-thirty-year veteran in the California State Park System told me recently that when he became a ranger, at least eight out of every ten rangers knew everything about what was in their parks. Now it was more like two out of ten. The people who pay their salaries deserve more than that!

As a retired teacher in park management at a California community college and a retired long-time seasonal ranger, I was in a position to watch this evolution over the years, so I wasn't particularly shocked. I was right in the middle of it all. I think that I have prepared for years to write a book like this.

Over the years I had worked for the National Park Service in Yosemite, one of America's most popular parks, and as a seasonal in the Santa Clara County (California) Parks, a large regional park system. In Yosemite, I was first a backcountry ranger and then went to the front country, where I was a protection ranger and was armed with almost full peace officer authority. I had moved from a more generalist ranger position to a special enforcement position. As a Yosemite seasonal, I was not able to investigate crime but certainly was able to make physical arrests and put people in jail. When I worked for the County of Santa Clara, I was not armed and had limited law enforcement authority.

I also spent five months as the "Acting Director" of the Santa Clara County Park System. The county borrowed me from the college as a full-time consultant while they looked for a new director. Santa Clara County has over 50,000 acres of parkland and over 200 employees in its Park Department. This experience was a huge part of my education. I sure learned about the how political process works.

In my position at West Valley College in Saratoga, California, I worked closely with those agencies that hired our people when they left college to start their careers. We had a program Advisory Committee that consisted of people from a large variety of park agencies. Included on that committee were members of the National Park Service (NPS), California State Parks, Santa Clara County Parks, Mid-Peninsula Open Space District, Town of Los Gatos, City of San Jose, City of Palo Alto, United States Forest Service, California Department of Forestry, and the California Land Management Company, a private agency. The committee included both field and administrative people, including a NPS Superintendent (Pinnacles National Park) and two park directors (Los Gatos and Santa Clara County).

Our program at the college also had a viable in-service training outreach to the entire West Coast. People from all over the western states came to our campus once a year for a week's training. The college also annually hosted a one-week Region Five Recreation Academy for the United States Forest Service.

Everyone, particularly those on the Advisory Committee, kept me abreast of what was happening in the field and made suggestions for adding or subtracting subject matter and curriculum so that our students were up to date on what was happening. As an example, we took park law enforcement in and out of the curriculum several times. We did decide to keep California State Penal Code 832 (832 P.C.), which was the minimum enforcement class that a person needed to complete for local seasonal employment and which was certified by the California Police Officers Standards and Training (POST).

At West Valley College, there was a class in every function of park management in the curriculum, from being a ranger to park maintenance. We also had a unique cooperative program with Santa Clara County. We used one of their parks (Sanborn County Park) as an invaluable practical laboratory and students were in it almost every day for "hands on" training.

I was the coordinator of the Administration of Justice, Court Reporting, and Park Management programs at West Valley when the college administration put the three programs together as a cost cutting measure. In that capacity, I created a survey of all park systems in California that employed rangers to ascertain what enforcement training they needed and then traveled to Sacramento to give the results to POST in an effort to get them to revise 832 P.C. I thought that this forty-hour training in the laws of search and seizure was just enough to get someone in trouble and park rangers needed much more. The survey listed all the POST Academy subjects and hours and asked which subjects their rangers needed in their positions at the agencies. The results of the survey recommended 193 hours of training instead of 40. It was about half the required training for fully armed peace officers. The subjects that the park agencies eliminated were those that enforcement traditionally did, like criminal investigation, traffic investigation, and firearm training.

Eventually POST did change 832 P.C., although my feeling when I left the meeting with POST was that they couldn't have cared less. They said that they were reluctant to start another academy just for rangers, and if the agencies wanted more enforcement training, they could come to POST. POST did take this problem to the University of California, Davis, for more study and 832 P.C. did get changed to 60 hours. A copy of the survey is in the Appendix of this book.

As I taught in the Park Management Program, with each ensuing year I began to observe that young people who were coming into the program wanting to be in the ranger professions were far less tuned to the environment around them than previous students. The old knowledge and skills that were expected from park rangers were starting to fade. I noticed, as well, that programs in four-year colleges and universities were also seeing a decline in the number of students who desired to become park rangers. A professor at one of those schools told me he suspected that the decline was because of a changing park culture toward law enforcement. People interested in a degree that included law enforcement were enrolled in Administration of Justice programs. In April 2013, I attended a meeting on how the college program that I had taught in for years could be saved from the axe. Not enough people were interested in careers in parks to make it pay for itself.

In my experience, most visitors expect rangers to have a sense of nature and the environment. To a park visitor, "a ranger is everything to everybody." Yosemite Backcountry Supervisor Roger Rudolph made that statement to our backcountry ranger group during a training session, and I never forgot it. That statement hung over the door of my classroom at West Valley College as a reminder so that every student who went out the door would see it. I have been told by one retired

National Park Service superintendent that it seems that statement might not be true anymore.

When I was a backcountry ranger in Yosemite, the Chief Ranger, Bill Wendt, once told our group of rangers that if we thought being a ranger was an 8 to 5 job, we were crazy! He was right; it wasn't. In the Yosemite backcountry, we worked 10 to 12 hours a day, but were only paid for eight!

In the backcountry I had to get up at dawn to find my horse and belled mule, give them their breakfast, then fix my own. I'd patrol all day (for the most part), take care of the stock before supper, and patrol local camping areas during supper time to see that people were keeping their food from bears. Then I got to fix my own supper, do my paperwork, and plop into bed. If people got lost, they were usually missed at the end of the day. There were times when I had been called out of bed in the middle of the night to solve a visitor's problems, like a medical emergency at Tuolumne Lodge or Washburn Lake, or a huge leak in a restroom that had water flowing downhill into peoples' tent sites at Tuolumne Meadows.

Even though rangers were paid an hourly wage, there was seldom any overtime or extra pay for what we did. It was just accepted as a part of our job. We had to be devoted. Although some state, county, and regional rangers lived in park housing, most rangers who worked in those agencies got to leave the park and go home every night. Rangers who lived in the park were on call 24/7.

Not only did rangers have to know the proper decisions to make during an enforcement situation, they needed to know how to clear a log off a trail, how to handle bears, where the good fishing was, where to go to have the best chance of seeing a variety of birds, what kind of flower or tree "that" was, and other information that would allow people to have a good park experience. The people who visited the park also expected us to have that knowledge. They took that knowledge for granted. It was the "traditional ranger image." Most rangers I worked with believed in that concept. Even today, most rangers in state, county, and regional parks still need to know how to identify a bay tree.

I personally believe that modern parks and park management could be heading for trouble. The population is growing and becoming more urban. The result is development closing in on park boundaries. There are more visitors to parks with no additional funding to meet the crunch. Open space and the money to purchase land are fast disappearing, and we have become so specialized that the true reason for rangers being in parks is becoming lost. More rangers are needed, but little money is available to hire them. Present generations are not outdoor people, like those in the past.

Most early park employees were drawn from agriculture. They grew up in a rural world, which is not at all true in the present day society. They already came to the profession with a background in nature and had to learn about law enforcement. Now it is just the opposite. People who are interested in coming into the profession are coming from an urban background and have to learn about the natural world.

This book will look at the historical past of parks, why we have them, and where we are right now in the evolution of the traditional role of the ranger in parks. I have added the historical evolution of parks because without the history and philosophy behind why parks are there and why we have them to protect, there would be no need for park rangers. Parks have been through an interesting evolution, and rangers are a huge part of that historic open space culture.

Because of the variety of my experiences, I felt that I was qualified to try to tell the story of how rangers have evolved in America. I have been deeply involved in issues around how to train a present day ranger and have actually experienced the transformation. I have been there, done that.

In order to put park issues into perspective, I sent out a small questionnaire to rangers I had worked with in the National Park Service and to some California state, county and regional park rangers and administrators. It went to a small select group. They all passed it on to others, both active and retired. It got around quickly because the interest in these topics was strong in our professional community. I asked them the following questions (my comments are in italics):

1. Was there any significant event or events or societal change that seemed to have caused the job of park ranger to evolve into "strictly" a law enforcement officer? *I was aware that the trigger was Yosemite's Stoneman Meadow Riot, but wanted to know if they were. All the National Park rangers cited this event, but very few rangers in other agencies even knew about the Yosemite riot.*

2. Do you feel that new people coming into the field lack outdoor skills and/or a land ethic necessary to be a good park ranger? *I should have asked them if new people knew about the environment in which they were going to work. Surprisingly, some folks did not think knowing this was even necessary.*

3. Is there any way that park management can turn this trend around, if it is indeed a trend? *Everyone agreed that it could not be turned around in the present management climate.*

4. Why did you become a park ranger in the first place? *Not surprisingly, almost all respondents said they did it because they loved the outdoors. One person answered that he wanted to do law enforcement.*

I attended the Annual California Park Training Conference in 2013, where I passed out another small survey. I needed opinions of field-level people now working in the profession. Most of those I had talked to before were retired. The results of the 2013 survey as well as the original survey are interspersed throughout this book and raw data from the 2013 survey appear in Appendix B. The survey did tell me that some rangers were more sensitive to protecting their parks than I had thought, which was not surprising in that the survey was compiled at a professional conference of mostly "generalist" or "traditional" rangers. The strictly "protection" rangers belonged to different organizations and many of those did not attend.

This book certainly is not a scientific study of what seems to be a change in the profession, nor is it a complete history of that evolution. I felt that modern rangers need to know that there is a history in their profession based upon a generalist culture that is still important today. My surveys have too few responses to be statistically significant and there are only a few responses from agencies outside of California, but I feel that the responses are a good indication of what is happening in our profession.

I found it difficult to remain impartial on some issues. My opinions ooze out in places. This book contains some of the attitudes, observations, and beliefs of park rangers who believe that change has been occurring in the profession, as well as responses from rangers who do not believe changes have happened. One ranger responded, "My gosh, are we going there again?"

I would hope that as you read this, you would picture a bunch of rangers sitting around a campfire after a day's work, discussing what is happening to the profession and what has happened to them in the past. We actually did that often in Tuolumne Meadows. There was a campfire almost every evening in back of the ranger station. I dearly hope that this book might capture the essence of those campfire chats.

Section 1

Growth of the Park Systems in America and the Issues Facing Parks in the Modern World

Yosemite's Half Dome (Photo by Edward Weiss)

Grizzly Giant, Yosemite National Park
(Photo by Violet Weiss)

Chapter 1: The Importance and Value of Parks and Open Space

Everybody needs beauty as well as bread, places to play in and pray in where nature may heal and cheer and give strength to body and soul alike.

John Muir

Parks can mean different things to people. For some, parks are avenues of escape from the stress of modern life. For others, they are places for high adventure and for organized activities, such as soccer and softball. Some even see parks as an avenue to make a living. We find all kinds of parks and open space to meet different needs, usually set aside and administered by government agencies and paid for by tax dollars. Because they are protected and managed by an interesting variety of agencies of government, they are often the brunt of budget cuts and cuts in services. They also are at the mercy of people in the seats of power, and pressures are sometimes brought to bear to change park management philosophy depending upon political ideology.

A survey done for The Nature Conservancy in 2012 revealed that even the fledgling Tea Party, an anti-big-government movement, agreed that parks should remain to be run by government and that taxpayer's money should be spent to keep them up.[1]

A flyer I received in the mail from the National Park and Conservation Association (NPCA) in March 2013 stated that even in a politically divided nation there is almost universal agreement about the importance of protecting our national parks. A survey by NPCA has shown that 81% of the voters had reported visiting a national park and wanting to visit one again in the near future.[2] There was almost 100% agreement that supporting parks was an appropriate role of government.

The voting public of my county has generously provided funding through the Santa Clara County Charter for land purchase and operations. The last renewal of the funding was passed with over 80% of voters agreeing to the commitment. That was a wonderful stamp of approval!

Parks are good for the economy

Parks, even at the local level, are targets for ecotourism and are an important part of this nation's and the world's economy. Consider what the average family might spend visiting a local, regional, state, or national park to camp or picnic or enjoy other outdoor recreation. Gas, food, lodging, and equipment are purchased from local stores and gateway communities. Not only is the National Park System responsible for $13.3 billion in local private sector economic activity an-

---

[1] Public Opinion Strategies, a letter from Lori Weigel to The Nature Conservancy on the results of an opinion poll taken by FM3 Associates, July 2, 2012.
[2] National Parks and Conservation Association, *Protecting Our National Parks, An Action Plan to Address Park Threats*, a mailing to members, March 29, 2013.

nually, it generates at least four dollars in value to the public for every tax dollar expended.[3] Yet when economic times are bad, parks are often the ones to take the monetary hits.

The Federal Government made huge cuts in the National Park Service's budget for the fiscal year 2013. Yosemite and Yellowstone, as an example, were cut over a million dollars in operations funding, affecting the number of seasonal rangers and other employees who could be there to serve the public.

Arizona has closed state parks and has turned over the management to local entities for several more. They are not alone.

When California discussed the closing of several state parks, one state senator who liked the idea was reminded of what would happen to the economy of his district if they closed a local state park. He changed his mind in a hurry. The park had a huge impact on the economy of the surrounding community. It was brought out during the discussion by state government to close some of the parks that California State Parks gave back $2.38 to the state for every dollar spent on parks in tax revenue from gasoline, food, and other items spent by park visitors. What other government agency does that? In the national parks, the return is even greater. NPCA reports that every dollar spent by government brings in $10, and for every two National Park Service jobs, one is created outside the Park Service.

I would like to think that most government officials understand that parks and ecotourism are a huge part of our economy and our daily lives and that most people love their parks and are willing to spend money to see them. If politicians do not, then our government is not paying attention or political ideologies are getting in the way.

In the fall of 2013, different ideologies got in the way when a dispute over the federal budget caused the government to shut down. The shutdown closed all 401 of the national parks. National parks, forests, and all federal lands used for recreation were closed up tight, even

---

[3] Repanshek, Kurt, "Placing Economic Value on National Parks," *National Parks Traveler*, December 2006.

when those lands were not funded. Those already camping or staying in the parks had 48 hours to get out.

The National Park Service attempted to close open plazas in Washington, D.C., which caused national attention when a group of veterans who had traveled to see the WWII Memorial were turned away by a park ranger. Seizing the opportunity, a member of the House pulled away the barricades and let them in. In a nanosecond, the incident, including the chiding of the ranger by the House member, was all over social media. Public opinion about the closings was openly hostile. The Department of Interior was deluged by phone calls from ordinary citizens citing missed opportunities and dollars spent on reservations, and vacations in ruin. The Department of Interior said that businesses lost $14 million per day.

Huge pressures were brought to bear from local and state governments to keep the parks open. The Governor of Arizona even threatened to send the National Guard to the Grand Canyon in an attempt to keep from losing tourist dollars. Eventually Arizona ended up paying the Federal Government to keep part of the Canyon open. In Utah, tourism in October usually brings in $100 million to the economy. When their parks were closed, Utah threatened to take over the ones located in their state by force. A deal was made to keep them open with Utah dollars. The Governor quickly wired $1.67 million to the Federal Government to keep them open. The Interior Department said that they would consider any agreement with a governor that would use state dollars to fully fund Park Service personnel in their states to re-open the parks located there. Local businesses outside of Grand Canyon even pledged $400,000 to re-open the park. Some states, however, did not have the money to do anything.

California's Governor refused to use state dollars to reopen just Yosemite, bad news for the nearby gateway community of Groveland, California, already hit by the effects of a large forest fire. In early August 2013, a huge forest fire that was human caused had broken out in the Sierra Nevada Mountains near Yosemite National Park. The fire burned over 200,000 acres and cost over $127 million to contain. Summer is the most important time for gateway communities to make their yearly profits. It is the time most people visit Yosemite and the other mountain open space attractions, so the cost to the economy was in the millions of dollars at a time when the communities were still recovering from a recession.

To Groveland, with just over 600 people, the fire was particularly devastating. One popular restaurant had to lay off 35 of their 45 employees, a huge number for such a small community. For most gateway cities on the edge of federal lands, the closing was a financial disaster of major proportions and some businesses throughout this country may never recover.

Of course taxpayers were caught in the middle. Defying the park rangers to arrest them, many scaled the fences, threw away barriers, and entered anyway. Through social media, fingers were pointed at both sides of this political failure.

Park personnel and other federal employees were furloughed, but promised back pay. Most people I know working in parks are on the edge financially anyway, and even if they are repaid, closures create a financial burden.

Looking at the glass as half full instead of half empty, there are some positives. Letting a park "rest" from heavy use is certainly one positive side. The biggest plus is that with all the media exposure, every person that is paying attention now knows how important parks are to the economy of this great country of ours.

Politicians sometimes use parks as a political football to get the voters' attention. Nothing gets a voter's attention more than when something that adds to their quality of life is no longer available. Closing parks had happened once before, when the Federal Government closed down for 28 days in 1995. You would think that politicians would remember.

When the economic woes got bad for government in California, politicians responded with a plan to close state parks as an "attention grabber." Not a single person has convinced me that closing parks saves money, not only because of the money given back in tax revenue or fee collection that is lost, but because of what happens to a park when no one is around to protect it. Maintenance often is deferred due to budget constraints, but when parks are closed maintenance issues become worse because of vandalism. Other crime problems may also arise. Mexican drug cartels, as well as other criminals, are waiting for the chance to plant their pot farms on public lands.

Recently the mission of California's Santa Clara County regional park system was under fire by a couple of members of the Board of Supervisors because they felt that some of their citizens were not using the parks, yet were paying taxes in support of them. Of course, that is also true of other agencies of government like hospitals, police, and fire protection. Those who wanted to "urbanize" the park system had little sense of what regional parks were all about. I think they also wanted to access the park's revenue source.

The county parks are a regional system and of such importance that they draw people to them from farther away than local neighborhood parks do. They are set aside for unstructured activities such as meditating, hiking, boating, cycling, camping, picnicking, or riding horses, as well as for the protection of open space and the biological diversity they contain. Because they are usually "natural," they protect the unique plants and animals indigenous to the area. Every ecosystem present in the county is protected somewhere in the Santa Clara County park system. I must admit that it just happened and was not by design.

There are always interest groups that want to use the parks for their own purposes and that lobby politicians. Only recently members of Congress, backed by the National Rifle Association, were trying to open all the national parks to hunting. The issue is still not decided. Park agencies always seem to be on the defensive to protect their mission.

Public Lands and Their Commercial Value

From the very beginning of "America's best idea," parks have been under fire from conservative political viewpoints. When Yellowstone was being considered to be our first national park, it had to first be looked at for its commercial value. As good luck would have it, Yellowstone was considered a wasteland by Congress. The primary resources, lodgepole pines, had little commercial value and still do not. Gifford Pinchot, a United States Forest Service (USFS) icon and its first director, thought parks were a huge waste of time and natural resources. Each time a park was thought to be of national value, infighting in government began over commercial values that led to bitter rivalries between the USFS and the National Park Service. A classic example was the fight over Crater Lake National Park in Oregon. The lake is 13,000 surface acres. The USFS just wanted to concede enough land to surround the lake. The National Park Service wanted more. The park ended up being larger than Yosemite at 183,000 acres and the result left bitter tastes in the mouths of USFS people that still linger.

The 2013 government shutdown brought out several suggestions from the conservative far right to sell some national parks. It has been a goal since the beginning of the 1970 Sage Brush Rebellion, a western conservative movement, to give the control of the federal lands to the states. In fact, James Watt, a lawyer for the movement, became the Secretary of Interior under Ronald Reagan. The sole purpose was to expedite oil and gas extraction from federal lands. The Federal Land Policy and Management Act of 1976 listed recreation as one of the multiple uses of public lands; transferring those lands to the states potentially threatened that multiple use philosophy.

Selling public lands to the highest bidder is another matter. There is already a mechanism for the Bureau of Land Management to sell public lands considered to be "surplus." The problem is defining what "surplus" means. Recent platforms for the Republican Party included items that would financially starve the National Park Service and other land management agencies in the Federal Government, hitting them in the pocket book and forcing them into selling or giving the lands to the states. It is not a fiscal thing, but an ideology that is driven by special interests. All this has led to a call from some really far right members of congress to sell or rid the Federal Government of national parks and other public lands as a way to solve our national debt problems. The fact is that the impact of national parks is very minimal and would not even make a dent in the debt. As mentioned earlier in this book, the "problem" of public land and what to do with ownership will continue to be a real concern when people with "nature deficit disorder" become the decision makers.

Each time governmental power changes in Washington and in state capitals and municipalities, parks either flourish or take financial blows from those people in power. When you are a ranger or a park administrator, you need to be very flexible to change.

Parks Promote Quality of Life

A very good park system can give a city and the surrounding community more than just the economic value in money given back in taxes. A well maintained park system is also a quality of life issue, because parks promote a sense of community and provide health and environmental benefits to the citizens. Parks can attract business, boost tourism that creates jobs, and put higher value on homes and businesses.

Many park systems provide concession services inside their parks in addition to protection and maintenance services. Facilities like hotels and restaurants, horseback rides, and ski areas found in large national parks and some state and regional parks are there because the government agencies, which do not want to put forth the money to run them, find them necessary to enhance a park visitor's experiences. These services provide income to the governing agency and jobs for the surrounding community.

Love for the Outdoors is in Our Genes

Behavioral scientists might tell you that in the human psyche there seems to be a gravitational pull toward nature. Noted biologist, E. O. Wilson, calls it "biophilia," or a tendency for humans to affiliate with life and lifelike processes.[4] Researchers have found that people of all cultures, when given the freedom to select where they would like to live, preferred two types of locations. One was a high place, where they could look far and wide over a park savanna with copses of scattered trees. The other was near a body of water, like a lake or stream.[5] Wilson says that these preferences have been passed on for generation to generation as far back as primeval times. Man would seek places to live that allowed protection of trees and height, a view of wildlife, and a place to obtain water. People around most urban areas seek such places as an urban/wildland interface in which to live. These areas usually have the most expensive homes, and few people can afford such property. Parks then become an escape into the natural world for most people.

Not only does it appear that the natural world is embedded in our genes, but in other aspects of our being. Psychologists have discovered that just a view of natural environments generates a feeling of tranquility, a decline in moods of fear and anger, and in some cases, even lowers blood pressure. Buildings often have offices that open into landscaped patios, because employees reported fewer feelings of stress and greater job satisfaction when they could look out their window at natural environments. A local company think tank located in the hills of Santa Clara County had a "cow cam" that employees can turn on so they can see something natural and to check if the cows are grazing on their property.

Architects often design buildings to bring the outside in. I told an architect to do just that when he designed a new room for our home.

An article appeared in the August 26, 2010, *San Jose Mercury News* about a University of Michigan study that revealed that people learned significantly better after a walk in nature, than after a walk in an urban environment. People buy small waterfall fountains for their soothing sound. The first director of the Santa Clara County Parks

---

[4] E.O. Wilson, *The Creation*, W.W. Norton, New York, New York, p. 63.
[5] Ibid, p. 66.

once told me that in order for a park to be successful, it had to have a water feature. To a park ranger, water plus people can equal trouble.

A Quiet World

After reading Douglas Brinkley's book, *The Quiet World*, about the creation of wilderness areas in Alaska, it came to me that there is another reason for natural parks and wildlands. Areas set aside as wildland parks are places of quiet. Most modern park planners today set aside a grove of trees in urban parks for that very purpose: a place where people can have some quiet reflection, away from the rat race that sometimes defines urban life. It is also an effort to give an urban population a taste of nature.

An escape to quietness is certainly one reason we set parks aside. After spending a summer in Yosemite's backcountry, my mind became tuned to the silence. I only heard the birds sing or the gurgle of a stream or the wind in the trees—so much so, that when I came back to an urban area, any noise, like a car passing by, drew my attention. Lying awake in the early morning, I used to be able to hear the singing of robins. In my neighborhood I fear that threats from free-roaming pet cats along with loss of nesting habitat have almost taken that away.

I was standing at a gas station in our local town. Heavy traffic was whizzing by in large numbers. I asked the station attendant how he could withstand all the noise. His answer was "What noise?"

To some people, parks are like temples. Places like Yosemite National Park, the cathedral redwoods, and oak woodlands that are found in my own county fill people with such awe that it is a religious experience just to visit there. When I was a ranger at Merced Lake in Yosemite, a good friend who spent summers at the High Sierra Camp showed me fern grottos and secret meadows, where shafts of light shone down upon wildflowers. They were awesome! Several of the regional parks in the San Francisco Bay Area have such fern grottos, and wildflowers are abundant in the springtime. The citizens need to know how lucky they are to live in a state like California that values its natural character and its open spaces.

A Place to Learn

At a California park conference some time ago, the keynote speaker was Dr. Gary Machlis, a science advisor to the National Park Service Director and a professor at the University of Idaho. Gary talked about what parks meant to him. He mentioned temples, along with other reasons why we have parks. He said that parks are places set aside for their natural diversity and their interest to science.

Bill Mott, former East Bay Regional, California State, and National Park Director once said that natural parks are the colleges and universities of our environment. It is best to study things natural in places natural.

Some antibiotics come from plants. Parks could also hold the cure for cancer or for AIDs. That is not a far-fetched thought. Many plants on this planet's open spaces have yet to be discovered and their benefits determined.

Nature Appreciation

Looking at scenery is not usually a popular activity for our younger generations. Young people are more prone to be involved in active pursuits like skateboarding, baseball, or soccer. Organized activities are taking precedence over unstructured outdoor play. Unless parents make a concerted effort to introduce their children to the outdoors, modern children will be less close to nature and lack the knowledge, experience, and ethics necessary to take care of the land.

An article written by Donna St. George of the *Washington Post* and published in the *San Jose Mercury News* on June 25, 2007, stated that there had been a 50% decline since 1997 in the number of children ages 9 through 12 that spend time in the outdoors in other than organized sports. That proportion has now dropped from 16% to 8% today. This research by Sandra Hofferth of the University of Maryland also showed an increase in computer and video game playtime and time spent watching television for the same age group. To people in the park profession, that trend is worrisome. In a few years, that generation will be controlling the environment we live in and it will be the source the park profession will draw from for new employees.

In a poll conducted for The Nature Conservancy in 2012, a very high percentage (82%) of the American people felt that children not spending enough time in nature was at least a somewhat serious problem. Fifty percent of the people thought it was a serious problem.[6]

"Nature deficit disorder" is a term used by Richard Louv when describing today's youth in his book, *Last Child in the Woods*. This book should be required reading by rangers, park administrators, park commissioners, and politicians. *Last Child* points to the danger of having future environmental decisions made by a generation of people who have not adequately experienced the outdoors. I am already seeing new park employees without a clue as to what they are protecting. It is extremely important that they have a passion for protection of natural land values, and that passion is usually gained from outdoor experiences rather than from a classroom.

Over the years, there has been a huge urbanization of America that makes the preservation of open space even more important. A very high percentage of people now live in urban areas, and outward development is encroaching upon all of our parks, whether regional, state, or national. Wildlife corridors that allow critters to migrate from one open space to another are being cut off by housing, shopping centers, highways, and freeways. Development causes parks to become "islands" in a sea that will eventually cause unhealthy wildlife populations due to genetic inbreeding. Mountain lions are beginning to appear in backyards, coyotes are roaming the streets in urban areas, and the deer are eating the roses. Present rangers often do not seem to know that the problem exists. It was not rated a high priority item in

---

[6] Weigel op. cit.

my survey in 2013. Perhaps that is also a reminder of our switch to urban culture.

Historical Value

Parks protect things cultural and are a reminder of our past. In fact, all parks have a history. Like the Smithsonian Museum saves America's artifacts, America's parks are the museums of the outdoors. Parks everywhere also contain historic and cultural history.

In Santa Clara County, California, the Alviso Marina County Park was once a very important gateway to San Jose during the times before and during the Gold Rush. Several of our county parks were once Spanish Land Grants, the mines at Almaden/Quicksilver provided mercury to the gold rush, and Mount Madonna was the home of a very famous cattle baron of the late 1800s, Henry Miller. The new Martial Cottle Park will concentrate on Santa Clara County's agricultural past. Santa Clara County was once called the "Valley of Heart's Delight" because of the huge number of fruit trees. Chitactac/Adams Park, in the southern part of the county, features Ohlone Indian cultural history complete with petroglyphs.

National and state parks have many places set aside for historical purposes. Just in the San Francisco Bay Area there are several: Mission San Juan Batista State Park, Petaluma Adobe, John Muir House, and Fort Point, Presidio of San Francisco to mention a few. The first public historic site was set aside in New York to commemorate the winning of the Revolutionary War.[7]

The parks and park agencies have their own history, and it is important for decision makers to understand it so decisions made to protect them and provide for them will be in the context of their history and mission.

---

[7] Robert O. Binnewies, *Palisades, 100,000 acres in 100 Years*, Fordham University Press, New York, 2001.

Chapter 2: A History of Parks and Public Open Space in America

People came to America because they felt that it offered freedom. They came to own land and to partake of the opportunities America presented. This trend still persists, with people arriving every day with the same dreams. The "American Dream" has always been to own property. We have always had a land obsession and have always championed property rights. One side of my family has some roots with the Amish, who came to America to have freedom from hate and oppression and the freedom to worship God in their own manner and by their own philosophy. The early immigrants who came to America found abundant natural resources. There were vast stretches of timber. It was said that the forests were so vast that a squirrel could climb up a tree on the East Coast and not have to get down until he got to the Mississippi River.

The Boston Common: America's First Park

As America was populated by Europeans, cities and towns were created, and the new citizens found that they needed pastures for their cattle and horses. Lands, called "commons," were set aside for public grazing. The common pasture belonged to everyone. The idea was brought to America from England, where tracts of grazing land were saved for the same purpose. However, as the years went by, the land's recreational value became apparent. People began to use them for picnics or to "get away from it all." In the early days of this country, even cemeteries were used for picnics. It was just a short trip in the buggy to well-kept lawns and flowers.

The Boston Common was created in 1634. It consisted of 50 acres of land that once belonged to William Blackstone, the first European to settle in Boston, and was later owned by the Puritan founders of the Massachusetts Bay Colony. Up to the 1830s it was used by people as a pasture for their cows, which led to overgrazing and what is commonly known as the "Tragedy of the Common." Eventually a grazing "carrying capacity" had to be determined to save the property. This land was used in many ways over the years, including as a campsite for the British during the Revolutionary War and a location for hangings and food shortage riots. An ornamental fence was placed around the property and some promenades were added. One promenade dated to 1728, Fremont Mall, was an imitation of St. James Park in London.

Saving Lands for Public Parks: A New Idea

Before lands could be set aside just for recreation, some attitudes needed to be changed. Most developed outdoor spaces were for the privileged class. Natural woodlands were for the use of royalty to hunt in. The Dark Ages had taught people that leisure was evil, that time spent doing anything other than work and worship was not acceptable. That philosophy followed the Pilgrims to America. For years, recreation activities were usually work-related, like plowing contests or corn shucking contests. The contests were to see who could pick rows of corn the fastest or who could plow the straightest row. Shucking was the method that was used before mechanical corn harvesters were invented. People would work rows of corn and pick the ears by hand, removing the shucks as they went.

Those work ethics were passed on from generation to generation. Biblical beliefs say that humans were put on earth to dominate the land and all its creatures and that the wilderness was dark and foreboding. Those attitudes had to be changed before people could convince themselves to preserve nature. It took the efforts of poets, artists, and writers to start the change.[8]

In 1791, as directed by President George Washington, Pierre Charles L'Enfant developed the city plan for Washington, D.C. The plan provided spacious parks, squares, fountains, walks, and broad tree-lined

---

[8] H. Duane Hampton, *How the U.S Cavalry Saved the National Parks*, Indiana University Press, Bloomington, Indiana, 1971.

avenues which are still there today providing openness and spacious-ness in one of the busiest capitals in the world.[9]

Writers Henry David Thoreau, James Fennimore Cooper, and William Cullen Bryant wrote about nature, nature's importance to people, and how man was so wasteful that we needed to start thinking about set-ting aside resources for the future. Thoreau also suggested setting aside natural preserves, in which "bear and panther and some even of the human race may still exist and not be civilized off the face of the earth."

Artist George Catlin visited the upper Missouri River Native Ameri-can tribes in 1832 and suggested that we save lands in a great park that would preserve the Native American and their way of life, "where the world could see for ages to come, the native Indian ... amid herds of elk and buffaloes." Artists like Catlin, were showing the American public, through art, the visual splendor of nature. It was Catlin who brought paintings of Yellowstone back to Congress and helped to convince them about the wonders of the place. In 1825, art-ist Thomas Cole painted the scenery of New York, Niagara Falls, and the Hudson River. He pointed out that most Americans had a love of nature, and that we needed to pay attention to saving some of it. Early photographers like William Jackson also contributed to bringing the wonderment of the scenery to government and the public.

The Yosemite Grant of 1864

In June of 1864, and in the middle of a terrible Civil War, President Abraham Lincoln signed a very historic act in the history of parks in America. The Act set aside the Yosemite Valley and the Mariposa Big Trees as public land. It was the first such legislative act ever passed by the Federal Government to set aside land for public use and enjoy-ment. The land was then ceded to the State of California and became that state's first state park. A few years later, in 1905, the land was re-

---

[9] Sam Alfano, "Forest Service Recreation Management, A Historical Per-spective," a paper delivered at the Pacific Southwest Region Recreation Academy, March 18, 1985, West Valley College, Saratoga, California.

turned to Federal Government control and added to a new national park that surrounded the Valley.

Urban Parks: Frederick Law Olmsted and the Urban Park Movement

William Cullen Bryant pointed out in an editorial in the *New York Evening Post* in the mid-1800s that during his quest for fresh air, he found it was no longer possible in a half-hour walk, for the city dweller to reach open country.[10] While the artists, poets, and writers sought to create a different perspective about saving nature and wildlands, it was an urban park that first opened the door to the creation of wildland parks in America. Although the Boston Common became a public park, it was the creation of Central Park in New York that brought parks to the forefront.

The idea to create Central Park came from several places, but evidence suggests that Robert B. Minturn was the first person to bring the park idea to the attention of the public. It seems that Minturn took a tour of Europe, and when he returned he wondered why America could not be like Switzerland, England, and France, which had nice places to walk and ride. He stirred up enough people interested in creating such a place that a meeting was held to discuss the idea.[11] It appears that the original suggestion to create a park came from Minturn's wife, Anna Mary Wendall, and the real "agitation" to create the park came from her and was carried through by her husband Robert.

Central Park had problems from the very beginning. A variety of reasons to set aside the land came from different sides and with different motivations. In their book on Central Park, Roy Rosenzweig and Elizabeth Blackmar cite that the park emerged to make money, put the city's cultivation on display, lift up the poor and refine the rich, retard and enrich commercial interests, improve health, and provide jobs.[12]

---

[10] Alfano, op. cit., p. 8.
[11] Roy Rosenzweig and Elizabeth Blackmar, *The Park and People, A History of Central Park*, Cornell University Press, New York, 1998.
[12] Rosenzweig, Blackmar, op. cit.

The park's financial troubles in the development years caused cutbacks in the development and in the salaries of employees. Things have not changed much in this modern era.

The creation of Central Park brought forth another individual into the historical park scene: Frederick Law Olmsted. Olmsted was an inspiring landscape architect. He was born in Hartford, Connecticut, in 1821 to well-to-do parents who introduced him to nature and nurtured the love for pastoral scenery that shaped his professional work.[13] His accomplishments in life led him to be called the "Father of American Parks."[14] He and his partner, Calvert Vaux, chose the term "landscape architect" to describe what they did as a profession. It is a term still used today by landscape professionals.

Olmsted became the head of the Yosemite Commission and a leader of the group that campaigned to save Niagara Falls. He supervised and co-designed Central Park. Central Park is still being used today in almost the same configuration as it was designed and built in 1858. It has been said that men on horseback patrolled the park in 1859.[15] Along with Vaux, Olmsted designed the first scenic parkway in Brooklyn in 1868. The City of San Jose, where I live, had its first land set aside for a "public square" by surveyor Chester Lyman in 1847 when the city was first laid out. That became Saint James Park in 1868 and it is now a historical landmark. It has been said that the park was designed by Olmsted, but there seems to be no real proof that he had done this park. If one was to look at the plan of the park, however, it is typically Olmsted. His designs are recognizable. Olmsted's biography written by Witlod Rybczynski makes no mention of Saint James Park in his listing of projects in Olmsted's lifetime.

---

[13] J. Douglas Wellman, *Wildland Recreation Policy*, John Wiley and Sons, New York, New York, 1987.
[14] Charles Beveridge and Paul Rocheleau, *Frederick Law Olmsted, Designing the American Landscape*, Rizzoli International Publications, Inc., New York, 1995.
[15] Douglas Morris, "Professional Opinion Paper-Renewing the Park Ranger Profession," one of a series of professional opinion papers provided by the Coalition of National Park Service Retirees, date unknown.

Olmsted designed more parks and recreation grounds than anyone had before him, and he did this without ever having the benefit of a formal college education.[16] His son, Frederick Junior, helped to draft the language for the bill that created the National Park Service and the mandate that the parks were to be "conserved for the use of future generations."

Almost every town and city in America now has at least one park, or system of parks, within its governmental jurisdiction. Most early parks had a common evolution. Government would set aside land outside the city limits, or on the very fringe. First used as pastures, they then became pleasuring grounds. The citizens liked to venture there for picnics. Development then grew around them, making them more accessible to the public. Set aside to get away from it all, they became places for more structured recreation, such as baseball, tennis, soccer, arboretums, and zoos. City governments again bought land outside the boundaries that became regional parks and nature preserves. Where local urban parks are designed for the neighborhood, regional parks serve a region where people visit from miles away. Now these regional parks are starting to become surrounded by development, creating a modern "crisis" in park management. Soon there will be no places to move out past the city limits.

Just prior to the Civil War, society drastically changed in America. Hand labor was being replaced by machines. Particularly in the North, the Industrial Revolution occurred in the early 1800s. As is usually the case, an event like war also changes things. Technological advances that make war easier to wage carried over to make life a little easier afterward. After the war, some of those advances made some people very financially comfortable.

After the Civil War, rich and upper middle class women were released from the mundane chores of keeping husbands happy and maintaining households. This change in their quality of life allowed them to turn to gardening and other outdoor activities. During the Progressive Era, from the early 1900s to the 1930s, women became in-

---

[16] Beveridge, op. cit.

creasingly involved in the outdoors and became important players in the conservation movement that was taking place through local, state, and national women's clubs. Women became an important bridge between male elite leaders and a wider audience.

Important Legislative Acts

Antiquities Act of 1906

There have been many legislative acts in government that have created parks and outdoor spaces all over America. Perhaps there has been none so important and powerful than the Antiquities Act of 1906. This law gave the President of the United States the power to restrict the use of lands already owned by the Federal Government and allows the President to set aside areas to protect historic and scientific objects.

This historical act came about because of the problem in some of the ruins in the Southwest because "pot hunters" were stealing Native American artifacts. Iowa Congressman John Lacey, then the Chair of the Public Lands Committee of the House was the prominent person behind the passage of this bill.

Since its passage, the bill has been used by many presidents, the first being President Teddy Roosevelt (Devil's Tower, Wyoming, in 1906) and recently by President Barack Obama (several during his term as President)

The Act has been revised twice yet has survived several appearances in the Supreme Court. The revisions were to require Congress to approve lands in Alaska and Wyoming when a president tries to set aside monuments in those states. Usually the challenges come as to the size of the area, as the Act says "the smallest area possible."

The Outdoor Recreation Resources Review Commission (ORRRC)

World War II gave us down sleeping bags and packaged, freeze-dried foods. After the war, the GI Bill allowed veterans to get a college education, which not only educated thousands of young people and gave better jobs and more money, but gave them more leisure time to enjoy the outdoors. Outdoor recreation exploded.

More leisure time, more dollars to spend, and a more mobile population began to impact parks and recreation areas nationwide. In 1958, Congress enacted Public Law (P.L.) 85-470 establishing a commission to determine the wants and needs of Americans as they pertain to outdoor recreation, determine what resources they would need to meet those needs, and predict the future. They did this through public meetings, education groups, labor groups, and public utilities. The law also established an inventory of what was now available and provided matching grants to states and federal agencies.

Several things came out of this politically-balanced commission that had support from President Eisenhower and later from President Kennedy. The Commission found that walking for pleasure and picnicking were the things Americans liked to do most and that there was a need to locate public lands closer to cities and towns. Any lands that had a base of water activities were also popular. The National Park Service responded in 1972 by creating Gateway East in New York, Cuyahoga Valley in Ohio, Santa Monica Mountains in Los Angeles, and the Golden Gate National Recreation Area on San Francisco Bay. Most of the lands in Golden Gate were already part of the Presidio of San Francisco.

The ORRRC was right. The Golden Gate National Recreation Area (NRA) has 13 million visitors every year. It is patrolled on one side of the Golden Gate by park rangers and on the other, more urban side, by United States Park Police. Golden Gate NRA is a first. When Congress created the park from federal lands, the mandate was that the new park be self-sustaining and operate without federal funding.

That became a reality in 2012 when it was announced that goal had been met.

The Commission suggested that several things should happen. Congress enacted laws from the ORRRC recommendations to create the Land and Water Conservation Fund, the Wilderness Act, the Wild and Scenic Rivers Act, and the National Trails Act. The Bureau of Outdoor Recreation (BOR) was established in the Department of the Interior to coordinate and provide technical assistance. The BOR's name was soon changed to the Heritage Conservation and Recreation Service (HCRS). This bureau was quickly dissolved by Interior Secretary James Watt at the onset of the Reagan Administration and the work was transferred to the National Park Service.[17] Of course, the popularity of recreating in the outdoors opened the doors to many agencies to hire rangers to protect people and the lands they use for recreation. Park rangers, usually associated with isolated areas, were now needed in more urban environments.

Land and Water Conservation Fund

Perhaps the most important legislation in support of outdoor recreation in America came from the Land and Water Conservation Fund Act of 1965. The Act was a bipartisan commitment to save natural and cultural history and to provide recreation opportunities to all Americans.[18] The fund has put over $900 million a year into the government coffers through taxes on offshore oil and outboard motor fuel, the sale of surplus federal lands, plus federal campground fees. The money is intended to create and protect national parks, forests, and wildlife areas and to provide matching grants to state and local communities throughout the United States on a 50/50 basis for acquisition and development of park land. However, it has never been funded at 100% because Congress and the President have used the funds for balancing the budget. As a result, the amount of money in the fund fluctu-

---

[17] George Siehl, "The Policy Path to the Great Outdoors, A History of the Outdoor Recreation Review Commissions," discussion paper prepared for the Outdoor Resources Review Group, October 2008.
[18] Bureau of Outdoor Recreation.

ates a great deal. The program has protected over 5 million acres of land and has provided over 3 billion dollars in grants over the years. The Act was first mandated to last only 25 years, but has since been extended to the year 2015.

The 1960s also saw the Forest Service benefit from the Multiple Use and Sustained Yield Act that gave outdoor recreation the same status as timber, mining, watershed protection, wildlife, and grazing interests. Backcountry "rangers" were hired to clean and patrol their wilderness areas, provide a more professional operation of campgrounds, and manage other recreational activities that occurred in the national forests.

Wilderness Act of 1964

It would be appropriate to mention wilderness when speaking of natural places like national, regional, and state parks, since much of the land in large parks in this country is set aside for naturalness, where people can find solitude and a "quiet world." Backcountry is the term used for most large natural areas in parks that are not developed and are accessible only by trail. Law enforcement is seldom an issue because of the difficulty of getting to and living in that kind of environment. It seems that the "bad people" do not want to put out the effort.

It is in wilderness or backcountry that generalist rangers are in the greatest demand. Education about saving the land for the future is foremost in the minds of rangers. A long way from logistical support like maintenance help and enforcement backup, wilderness rangers make do with what they have. If something breaks, they fix it! Enforcement situations, usually resource based, are handled at the lowest effective level. It is rare that a ranger has to take anyone into custody. It would be a very long hike out to the trailhead.

The preservation of wilderness in America came when there was some alarm at how land was being exploited in the move west. It also followed the development of our sense of values. The first thought was only about preserving geological features, like those found in Yellowstone, in Yosemite, and in the Grand Canyon. Then the idea developed that we ought to preserve plants and animals as well. It soon became accepted that we should preserve, for all time, certain parts of parks and forests that had not yet felt the "touch of man." This was a relatively new concept, since for centuries wilderness had always been viewed as something dark and mysterious.

The first real effort to set aside wilderness in America came during the 1920s from people like Bob Marshall and Aldo Leopold who were, at the time, United States Forest Service employees. Marshall became a champion for wilderness and wild areas in America. Leopold became one of the major wildlife biologists in this country when he later taught at the University of Wisconsin. As a result of their efforts, in 1939 the Forest Service was the first to set aside areas where there were to be no roads, cutting of timber, or commercial development.

In the 1970s, in what I call the "environmental era," when interest in the outdoors was high, backpacking and the use of wilderness and backcountry became viable leisure time pursuits. Soon some backcountry areas were starting to feel the impact of too many people. Wood for a campfire was difficult to find at the end of the summer season. The white bark pine, found in altitudes over 9000 feet in Yosemite, depended upon downed and decomposing wood. This adversely affected the population of these trees. Yosemite banned campfires over that altitude.

In 1964, a Wilderness Act that defined what wilderness should be was enacted through the efforts of the Sierra Club and similar organizations. This Act said that wilderness should be a place where there is no imprint of humans and where a person is only a visitor and does not remain. Also, there also should be an "essence" of wilderness in its setting and it should be more than 5000 acres in size. It should be large enough and isolated enough that human imprints are nowhere to be seen, even from the tallest peaks. There was to be a feeling of complete isolation. Wilderness and park backcountry are the last bastions of the traditional old-time ranger, the ranger that could do all of the duties in their description plus "all other duties as required."

The USFS management of wilderness is left to the Forest Supervisor. Three Sisters Wilderness, near Bend, Oregon, was one of the better-managed wildernesses that I have visited. It was well signed, and sanitation problems were solved by small "one-holers" located just off trails. The next time I was in that wilderness, those toilets were gone, as well as the signs. The new boss had said, "No imprint of man."

Civilian Conservation Corps (CCC)

No history of parks and open space in America is complete without mention of the contributions attributed to the Civilian Conservation Corps, which was created in 1933 during the first 100 days of President Franklin Roosevelt's first term and ended in 1942. The Corps was created to put people to work because the country was in a deep recession and many people were out of work. Thousands of young people, aged 17 to 24, were enlisted to serve. It was a military atmosphere where enlistees were paid $30 a month, housed in barracks, and served three meals a day. Most sent a large portion of that $30 home to family. In Arizona alone, they planted seven million trees, built miles of new trails, and built campgrounds, ranger stations, and 5700 miles of roads, mostly in open space. They completed 250 projects in the Grand Canyon alone.[19]

In California, they built campgrounds, trails, and supporting facilities like restrooms. In the United States Forest Service over 50% of the roads and trails provided by the Corps are still in use today.[20] California's Big Basin State Park was the site of a CCC camp and the mess hall is now the visitor center for the park. In fact, eight states in this country that did not have a state park system started one to take advantage of the CCC program.

---

[19] Kathy Montgomery, "Corps Values," Arizona Highways Magazine, March 2013, Volume 89, No.3, p. 44.
[20] Alfano, op. cit.

Chapter 3: Land Agencies That Protect Our Outdoor, Cultural and Historic Heritage

The National Parks: America's Best Idea

Alfred Runte, a historian who concentrates on national parks, stated that without parks, our country would be haphazardly developed and that we have at least developed a conscience about what we should and should not do to the land.[21] Our vast open spaces and the scenic vistas of the early years of our country have served us well.

Artist George Catlin was the first to suggest setting aside some of those large land areas as parks. In 1832 he suggested that we should preserve the wildlife and the Native American in a "grand national park"! As explorers traveled to the lands beyond the Mississippi, they brought back to the East strange tales of lands where steam erupted from the earth creating strange forms and mud pots boiled in the ground. Most of those early mountain men were known for their tall tales, so hardly anyone gave those reports any thought. Soon, enough reports had been made that the government had to find out the truth and launched a government-supported expedition into Yellowstone that included David Folsom, Henry Washburn, and Ferdinand Hayden. This expedition, organized in 1869, confirmed the rumors that such a place really did exist.

In 1870, another expedition of prominent citizens, the Washburn, Langford, Doane Expedition, entered the area that would become Yellowstone National Park. During that trip, one of the members, Judge Cornelius Hedges, suggested that the area be made into a national park.[22] This expedition eventually resulted in the creation of Yellowstone National Park in 1872 as a "pleasuring ground for the people." Nathaniel Langford became the first Superintendent but had no

---

[21] Alfred, Botkin Runte, Daniel, "Guest Column: Science, Open Space, And The Future of Our National Parks," *National Park Traveler*, November 26, 2012.

[22] J. Douglas Wellman, *Wildland Recreation Policy*, John Wiley and Sons, New York, 1987.

budget or laws to enforce. The United States Cavalry was sent to provide protection and stayed until the creation of the National Park Service in 1916. Like today, the Department of the Interior was the controlling agency. Many of those cavalry members transferred into the new agency and became the first national park rangers.

Federal Agencies

National Park Service (NPS)

The creation of Yellowstone started a drive to create and save areas of our country that had national interest. Taking care of Yellowstone and the other areas set aside soon became a thorn to government. It was almost like, "Now that we have them, now what?" Yosemite Valley and the Mariposa Big Trees had been ceded to the State of California in 1864 but what to do with Yellowstone became a dilemma.

The story was told that Twenty Mule Team Borax owner Steven Mather wrote a letter to then-Secretary of the Interior, Franklin Lane, complaining about the condition of the National Parks. Lane told him that if he didn't like it, he should come back and handle them himself. Horace Albright, then working in the Department of Interior at the request of Adolph Miller, a former professor at the University of California, said that Mather was really recruited to a position in government that included responsibility for the parks, a hospital for the insane, territorial problems, the Bureau of Education, and a variety of other activities. He was told, however, that parks would be his major concern. Mather did write the letter, but it was really Mather's interest in saving Yosemite's Hetch Hetchy Valley that brought him into contact with Secretary Lane. Albright was running the parks in those first years as part of his duties in the Department of the Interior. Mather was trying to convince the Administration that parks had to be a separate agency. Through the hard work of both Mather and Albright, the National Park Service was created on August 26, 1916. An excellent history of this process is covered in Albright's book, "*Creating the*

National Park Service," co-authored with his daughter and published in 1999 by the University of Oklahoma Press.

Park rangers, as part of a real park agency, soon followed the formation of the Service. The National Park System has grown over the years by leaps and bounds.

Many new "natural" parks were added, and the government also passed on the supervision of the national battle fields, the national cemeteries, and other historic sites to the new Park Service.

As a result of people stealing artifacts from Native American lands, President Teddy Roosevelt pushed through the Antiquities Act of 1906. Roosevelt was then able to create new National Monuments, because the Act allowed the President, through decree, to preserve places of scientific interest. Since then, each president, as part of his legacy, liked to designate a National Park System unit using this Act. The creation of a national park, however, can only be done by an act of Congress. As the years went on, national lakes and seashores were added to the system, as were recreation areas and urban parks like Golden Gate National Recreation Area in San Francisco and Gateway East in New York City.

As of this writing, the National Park System now protects 84 million acres of land that includes over 4 million acres of ocean beaches, lakes, and reservoirs, 85,049 miles of rivers and streams, 68,561 acres of archeological sites, and over 43,000 miles of shoreline. They also have over 121 million historical objects in museums and visitor centers. They now employ over 28,000 people. For the most part, rangers in the National Park Service have evolved into law enforcement and protection rangers. Most field positions in the NPS are now specialized positions.

Bureau of Land Management (BLM)

The Bureau of Land Management is another federal land management agency within the Department of Interior that has rangers. They administer 253 million acres of public land, mostly in the western states. BLM was created mostly to administer grazing leases and manage grasslands. Most lands are "surplus" lands in a recreational sense, as most of the scenic and historic land and lands with commercial value were already in the National Park System or the United States Forest Service. A large amount of BLM land is the Great Basin Desert in the western states. The BLM roots go back to the Land Ordinance Act of 1785, which provided for the survey and settlement of lands in the original 13 colonies and the disposition of land as our country grew westward. Today, BLM controls the recreation on over 200 thousand miles of fishable streams, 4500 miles of trail, and 2.2 million acres of lakes and reservoirs. Uniformed law enforcement rangers enforce the rules and regulations governing federal lands, as well as some state laws. Sometimes their jurisdiction is cloudy because of the many shared boundaries. The rangers' enforcement positions can be dangerous at times because of the role of protecting our borders with Mexico.

Corps of Engineers (COE)

The Army Corps of Engineers traces its origin back to the American Revolution when the Continental Congress first created an army. The Corps, part of the Department of Defense, manages more than 11.5 million acres of land and water for public recreation. Uniformed park rangers patrol the public land and reservoirs and provide law enforcement and public safety, natural, cultural, and historical resource management, and give interpretive programs. They are certainly the generalist rangers in public land management. Historically, when the COE would build a reservoir, the public would want to use it for recreation. COE would offer the facility to the national parks or to a state or local jurisdiction. If those agencies did not want to take on the management, then the Corps had to do it. I believe they got into the ranger business by default. Some of the facilities that they manage may have several different police radio frequencies because of their shared boundaries with other state and local jurisdictions.

Bureau of Reclamation (BOR)

The Bureau of Reclamation was established in 1902 and is part of the Department of the Interior. The agency builds dams for irrigation and for power throughout the Western United States. Twelve of those projects have been designated as National Recreation Areas managed by the National Park Service and the Forest Service. Like the Corps of Engineers, they sometimes operate recreation facilities on selected sites. Lake Berryessa in Northern California is a classic example of one project. Rangers hired by the Bureau give interpretive programs, manage the land and water resources and a large developed campground, in addition to providing limited law enforcement.

United States Forest Service (USFS)

The United States Forest Service manages 91.6 million acres in this country in 155 national forests and 20 grasslands that get subjectively a billion visitors a year. Their management philosophy is that of multiple use, of which recreation is only a part. The other parts of that management philosophy are timber production, wildlife habitat, watershed protection, grazing, and mining.

Forest reserves were first created in 1891, but were very restricted as to who could use them. When citizens went into a National Forest Reserve, they were literally trespassing. For that reason, "forest rangers" were created to patrol the forests. Because people wanted to use the forests to camp and hike, Congress passed a law in 1899 that allowed the recreational use of forest reserves. The Forest Service was created in 1905, but the Director, Gifford Pinchot, did not think much of either the national parks or the recreational use of his forests. It has been said that Pinchot had backed the damming of Hetch Hetchy Valley in Yosemite just to get back at the Park Service for locking up resources. He had the willing ear of President Teddy Roosevelt, as well.

Facilities like campgrounds or other development in the forests were pretty much left to hunters and anglers. Forests located near large cities, like Los Angeles, were beginning to feel the pressure to open for recreational use. The building of roads to access timber also opened the forests to use. It soon got to the point that the USFS could no longer ignore the public when it came to opening the forests to recreational use. The first modern campground was built at Eagle Creek in Oregon National Forest in 1916. Many more facilities were built in national forests by the Civilian Conservation Corps during the Roosevelt Administration in 1933.

The Forest Service also manages many wilderness areas in their system and thousands of miles of trails. Because national forests are not parks and because of their multiple use management, recreation is sometimes just tolerated.

For years any enforcement problems were handled by the local sheriff. Soon, even the sheriff was overcome by too many incidents in campgrounds and trails, even though USFS timber sales provided funding to local sheriff's departments. The USFS needed to provide their own enforcement program, even though the local sheriff still had jurisdiction. Level 5 Enforcement Officers have parallel duties to a park ranger. They not only enforce the law and conduct educational programs, but also assist local authorities in search and rescue. Forest Service personnel are not immune to the dangers that confront rangers when on duty. In 2011, Enforcement Officer Chris Upton was shot and killed in Georgia when mistaken for game by a hunter.

The Tennessee Valley Authority (TVA)

The TVA was created in 1933 as one of President Franklin Roosevelt's New Deal programs. The purpose of TVA was to improve the economic and social conditions in the Tennessee River watershed that covered 41,000 square miles. The program built 28 flood control dams that created places for people to recreate. Like the COE and the BOR, the policy of the TVA is for other agencies to take over the management and development of recreational facilities. Lands were turned over to the National Park Service, the United States Forest Service, state parks, and local agencies. However, TVA does manage over 238,000 acres of land. The Authority is also looking at turning lands over to commercial enterprise for management. The TVA owns over a million acres of land, in which over 400,000 acres of land and water is open to the public.[23]

United States Fish and Wildlife Service (FWS) and Other Wildlife Agencies

The Fish and Wildlife Service is a federal agency found in the Department of Interior of the U.S. Government. It oversees 560 wildlife refuges that contain over 150 million acres. They employ approximately 9,000 people. The organization originated in 1871 as the United States Commission on Fish and Fisheries when Congress noticed a decline of food fish. In 1885, the Division of Economic Ornithology and Mammalogy was created and then renamed to the Division of Biological Survey in 1896. In 1940 those two agencies mentioned above were combined and the FWS was formed.

The FWS has a mission to enforce federal wildlife laws, protect endangered species, manage migratory birds, and restore fisheries and wildlife habitat. One of the biggest things that they do is gather and distribute millions of dollars of excise taxes on hunting and fishing equipment to state wildlife agencies. Many state refuges, such as the Shasta Valley Wildlife Area in Northern California, are fully funded by this program.

The FWS does a lot of cooperative work with state fish and wildlife people as well as other government agencies. In our county, the FWS along with the California Department of Fish and Wildlife, our county and local cities, created a landmark habitat conservation plan for the Coyote River Corridor. This plan provided a framework for protecting and recovering 46,500 acres of habitat for endangered plants and animals in mostly an urban setting. Our local county park department manages the corridor that includes trails and buffers for the riparian areas.

---

[23] Robert Marker, and H. Ken Cordell, principle investigator and editor, *Outdoor Recreation in America, A National Assessment of Demand and Supply Trends,* Sagamore Publishing Company, 1999, p. 70.

All states have some kind of agency that manages fish and wildlife. In California, the protection of wildlife and fish goes back to 1830 when the Territorial Legislature discovered that "mountain men" were "illegally" hunting. In 1851 the first laws specifically aimed at fish and game matters were enacted.[24] At first concerned with the plight of oysters, it soon protected elk, antelope, deer, quail, mallards, and wood ducks. In 1871 two full time wardens were appointed, one warden to patrol San Francisco Bay and the other at Lake Tahoe. This warden force was expanded to 73 by 1907. Now several hundred wardens patrol the state. Game wardens patrol the refuges, enforce the law, and have almost the same duties of today's specialized park enforcement rangers. In fact, fish and game wardens are intertwined in the culture of park rangers. The protection of fish and wildlife, natural land values, protection of endangered plants and animals, and the education of the public about environmental issues, are all shared by both rangers and wardens.

State Parks in America

The iconic author George Perkins Marsh published the first book on land management written in English. His book, *Man and Nature,* was published in 1864. Perkins learned about land management when he served as a minister to Italy. He was able to see what the ancient Romans had done to ravish the land and was concerned that the United States was really headed that direction, as well. Marsh brought to the forefront what was happening to the Adirondack Mountains, which led to having that area set aside in the late 1800s.[25]

Early in the history of the National Park Service, Director Steven Mather was besieged by requests to create new parks. Those requests, in Mather's mind, were not even close to lands of national importance. National significance to Mather meant that someone who

[24] "Department of Fish and Games Celebrates 130 years of Serving California," *Outdoor California*, November-December, 1999.
[25] Karl Jacoby, *Crimes Against Nature*, University of California Press, Berkeley, California, 2001.

lived in Indiana, as an example, would want to make the effort to visit a park in Wyoming.

Mather felt that there ought to be some kind of cooperation between the Federal government and state governments to create a great "national system" of parks. He gathered members of the states to a meeting in Des Moines, Iowa, in 1921. Mather picked Iowa because he wanted the state to be in the spotlight because of the progress they had made on their park system. Iowa had ranked fourth in terms of the numbers of parks.[26]

The Des Moines meeting numbered 200 people. More than half were from Iowa. The meeting was actually billed as the first National Conference on Parks and not the first National Conference on State Parks as is often stated.[27] It was attended by a large variety of individuals and organizations including the Sierra Club, members of the General Federation of Women's Clubs, bird watchers, scientists, and wildflower preservation societies.

At the meeting when the roll was called, they discovered that 29 states had no state park system at all, and that six states had only one park. California only had Big Basin Redwoods State Park and some historic sites like Marshall Gold Discovery and Sutter's Fort. New York had set aside Adirondack State Park in 1892. In New York State, six million acres were included in the Adirondack mountain area.[28]

Mather looked at state parks as a "second tier" of a nationwide system of parks. Some in attendance at the conference were not too pleased with that assessment. Arguments went on for several years about what state parks should be. Would they be playgrounds for outdoor recreation or set aside for scenery or even for scientific reasons? As stated, the availability of the CCC during the Great Depres-

---

[26] Rebecca Conard, *Places of Quiet Beauty: Parks, Preserves, and Environmentalism*, University of Iowa Press, Iowa City, 1997.
[27] Rebecca Conard, "*The National Conference on State Parks, Reflections on Organizational Genealogy*," *The George Wright Forum*, Volume 14, Number 4, 1997, p. 28.
[28] Robert O. Binnewies, *100,000 Acres in 100 Years*, Fordham University Press, New York, 2001.

sion actually caused eight states to begin a state parks system.[29] One thing was certain. The states did not want to be told what to do by the National Park Service!

The result of this meeting was the creation of the "National Conference on Parks," which soon became the National Society for Park Resources, a function of the National Recreation and Park Association.

State governments are now among the major providers of outdoor recreation resources in this country. Each of the fifty states has at least one agency with the responsibility for outdoor recreation, parks, and the rangers who protect them. There are now almost eight thousand state parks in this country that have served over 750 million people a year, and they have added more than 20 billion dollars to the nation's economy each year.

Mather said, "Who will gainsay that the parks contain the highest potentialities of national pride, national contentment, and national health? A visit inspires love of country, begets contentment, engenders pride of possession, contains the antidote for national restlessness. He [sic] is a better citizen with a keener appreciation of the privilege of living here who has toured the nation's parks."[30]

Regional and County Parks

Regional and county park systems are an important link between urban parks and state parks. Usually larger than an urban park and more natural, they are designed to draw people further away from the urban community. Urban parks usually consist of a small park for the same area that serves an elementary school, and a larger park for the same area that serves a high school. The larger parks usually have tennis courts, baseball and softball diamonds, and other athletic facilities. Regional parks provide areas for camping, picnicking, hiking and equestrian use, sailing/boating, educational use, and unstructured

---

[29] Conard, op. cit. p. 29.
[30] Conard, op. cit.

recreation. These parks usually are more passive and natural in character.

When I first taught biology in a high school outside Phoenix, Arizona, I often visited Maricopa County's parks. Maricopa County has one of the largest regional open space agencies in the country, with 120,000 acres for people to enjoy. The parks offered examples of desert plants and animals native to Arizona, important for a biology teacher who grew up and was educated in Indiana.

The Growth of Regional and County Parks

The year was 1930. Thousands of acres of land on San Francisco Bay's eastern foothills already owned by the public had been set aside for water storage. The East Bay Municipal Utility District was receiving water from the Sierras and the utility no longer needed space for future dams for water storage. It did not take long for the public to see the recreational potential of those lands. There was a gathering at the University of California, Berkeley, of people who had shown interest in the formation of a park district. Ideas were shared and a study was done by Olmsted Landscaping Firm and Ansel Hall, a National Park Service planner, to consider the potential of such a use of the utility district's lands. The result was the formation of the East Bay Regional Park District in 1934.[31]

Because the new district encompassed more than one county, approval had to be made by the California State Legislature. The former mayor of Oakland, Frank Mott, drafted a bill that created a new regional park district and authorized a governing board. It was the first such law of its kind in the country. The District now has 65 parks, 1200 miles of trails, and 112,000 acres of parkland covering two counties.

---

[31] Frederick Olmsted Jr. and Ansel Hall, *Proposed Park Reservations for East Bay Cities (California)*, first published by a grant from the Kahn Foundation in 1930. Reprinted by the East Bay Regional Park District in 1984.

Calero County Park in Santa Clara County, California.
(Photo by the author)

In the early 1920s and '30s, counties all over the country began to set aside regional parks. Santa Clara County bought its first regional park property in 1924, followed by another purchase in 1927. Those two parks were maintained by prisoners from the county jail. Then the county purchased over 50,000 more acres and 24 more parks to make it one of the largest county park systems in the country. Over the past 14 years the regional park system in County of Santa Clara had an average of 2.4 million visitors a year.

In 1946, a Santa Clara County grand jury reported that the present number of parks in the county was inadequate to serve a growing county population. It also suggested that a new department be created. In 1955 a recreation commission was created to advise the Board of Supervisors on how to move toward meeting the Grand Jury's suggestion. A new department was created and soon after a new director was hired to manage the newly formed district in April 1957. The County now employees a large group of generalist rangers who enforce the law, do resource management projects, and give interpretive talks.

The country's tenth largest city, San Jose, California, has one large regional park. Alum Rock Park was carved out of lands that were a part of the Spanish Pueblo of San Jose. San Jose, then just a settlement, was entitled to 4 leagues of public land when it was a part of the Pueblo. The land was given back to the City by an act of Congress in 1851 in a settlement of land claims. This popular park, one of California's oldest municipal parks, is now over 1000 acres and is almost completely surrounded by homes.

Public parks and park agencies are all created by governmental action. One way the process begins is that someone has an idea for creating a park, approaches their local legislator about that idea, the person or a group lobbies for the creation of the facility, a law is brought forth to the legislative body, and it is either passed or rejected. The created park is left with a legal mandate that is usually included in the legislation. It is the American way.

Chapter 4: Politics and Parks

Legislative Mandates and Missions

Any agency created or managed by government is at the mercy of politics, elected politicians, and undue pressures from outside groups. Those pressures are also the American way.

A mission statement is a guideline on how an agency is supposed to be managed. For the National Park Service, the mission is to preserve the wildlife, scenery and historical objects, yet allow use of the same by such manner and such means as to leave the parks unimpaired for the enjoyment of future generations.

For my local park agency, the mission is to "provide, protect and preserve regional parklands for the enjoyment, education, and inspiration of this and future generations." The county park mission was developed by park staff and approved by both the Park and Recreation Commission and the Board of Supervisors. Santa Clara County Department of Parks and Recreation was created in 1957, and it took almost 50 years before the department created a mission statement.

The State Parks of California's mission is "to preserve the state's biodiversity, protecting its most valued natural and cultural resources and creating opportunities for high-quality outdoor recreation."

The State of New York's mission is "to provide safe and enjoyable recreation and interpretive opportunities for all New York residents and visitors and be responsible stewards of our valuable natural, historic and cultural resources." The statement continues on to give some guiding principles as a pledge to the folks that they serve. One of those commitments is a commitment to preservation for future generations.

Indiana, the state where I grew up, has a unique mission that includes both preservation and multiple use "while sustaining the integrity of these resources for current and future generations."

Almost all mission statements I have ever read have certain key elements. Those elements are to protect and preserve for future generations. I believe that all activities that take part in parks must meet the requirements of their mission statement. Everyone on staff at the parks, including the park planners, resource managers, the maintenance and protection staff, and the administration must support the mission with their actions and policies. The mission should have the complete backing of the political factions of government as well. It is the political factions that are the most worrisome. They have the ability to hire and fire employees, and in a more urban situation, elected officials might not have the understanding of what naturalness and parks are all about, and they might not even care.

Park directors and administrators need to be able to make decisions that give nature some rights, even though it might not be a politically popular thing to say or do. Saying that is easy, but doing it is difficult. Decisions that are political could cause transfer or the loss of a job. It is also unfortunate that term limits serve to get rid of educated governors, legislators, board members, and other really competent elected public officials who champion parks. The loss of those kinds of people in government causes park agencies everywhere to have to hope that new officials can be educated.

I was once told by the first director of our local county park system that his job was not to run parks (his second in command did that), but to get the money and keep the Board of Supervisors happy. That is a sad statement for a professional park manager to make. However, he did last 25 years as director.

Most park employees have experienced the frustration of knowing that in certain park management decisions they are right professionally and scientifically, but are wrong politically. There have been so many issues involving park management and politics that it would be hard to single out any one as an example, but since grazing rights are a big issue in the western states, I will use that as an example.

Much of the land in our local country park system was purchased from local ranchers. Obviously, when land is purchased for a park, it is changed from a consumptive use to a preservation use. The ranchers did not really want to take the purchase money and disappear, but wanted to continue to use the land to graze their cattle using the same methods as before. The parks also wanted to use cattle, but in a way that managed the resources wisely.

The ranchers had a great deal of political pull with some members of the Board of Supervisors. After many meetings and input from all sides of the issue, grazing permits were issued under some environmental constraints, and grazing plans for each park were created by grazing professionals and approved by the Board of Supervisors. In fact any new property purchase that has grazing possibilities must have a professional grazing plan done by a consultant. Some of the above constraints include numbers of cattle and periods of grazing. Of course, some of the ranchers did not agree with the grazing plans and getting a compromise took a lot of effort. Some of the ranger field personnel in parks did not like the idea of cattle grazing taking place on park land and that did not help matters.

Cattle grazing can help a great deal in resource management. Yellow star thistle is an invasive plant that is prominent in California. Grazing can help parks to rid itself of yellow star thistle when the plant emerges from the ground, but the cattle must be removed at the proper time to let other plants grow and shade out the star thistle. Grazing also helps control accidental fire in the absence of prescribed fire programs that are a political hotbed and somewhat risky. The "put cattle on, take cattle off" philosophy does not set well with some ranchers. It is hard for them to make money when they continually have to move their cattle around from one pasture to another.

In a classic example of local politics, one rancher's grazing lease ran out and the park system opened the permit to bids for the renewal of the grazing permit. After a long interview process, the permit was given to another rancher whose cattle had grazed on parklands for another agency outside the county and who had given more holistic answers during the screening process. The original rancher, who lost the bid, complained to a member of the Board of Supervisors who pulled the lease before it could be approved and got the board to approve new guidelines that only allowed the bid to be given to a rancher who resided in the county. The new rules threw the process back open, and the original rancher, now knowing what answers to give and what the parks wanted, had the right answers the second time. The original grazer got the bid the second time around. The whole thing resulted in a huge hourly loss by parks in their effort to be honest and fair.

Agency Missions Will Be Tested

As I have stated, most agency missions include the words "protect and preserve for future generations." Most park departments see this as a mandate to restore their parks to "what they once were before the white man appeared." It again points out the necessity of having rangers and field staff that have a finger on the pulse of their parks so that they can act as the eyes and ears of management or intervene with what is happening.

Many of our natural parks and open spaces are managed by keeping our hands off and what happens, just happens. We just let nature do her thing. I also might add that there are rarely truly natural open spaces anymore. Added to that is the problem of describing what "natural" means. We throw that word around when we speak of resource management and the duties of park rangers. We define parks that are "natural" as being those parks where nature is allowed to be in charge. If fires start in a natural way (lightning) and they do not threaten property, we let them burn. When floods occur, we let the land recover without intervening. If bark beetles attack the trees, it is nature's way, and we do not spray. As long as a dead tree does not have a target, it is left standing as a snag for insects and birds to use. It is easy to say those things, but it is often difficult to let nature have her say. Most traditional park rangers are there to protect the park's resources and to "manage" them. If a ranger is lucky enough to work for a progressive park agency, resource management is a priority item. However, most agencies try to keep things as they "once were" or to keep the status quo.

Humans have been around too long. Wildlife species once abundant in most areas are either extirpated or down to lower levels than they once were. Those that have been able to adapt like the coyote or in some areas, deer, become pests. Invasive plant species and animals are now present. Strict adherence to the mission of some park agencies is going to create a huge dilemma as things change as the belt tightens around existing habitats. Do we artificially introduce new gene pools as encroachment gathers steam? When do we intervene with the "natural way" of managing our wildlife and our park landscape?

As I have stated, some agencies have already brought in outside gene pools when wildlife were in trouble. It happened in California State Parks and in the East Bay Regional Park District when deer began to show signs of inbreeding. Both instances created controversy. People like to come to parks to see wildlife.

In the winter 2014 issue of *National Parks Magazine*, an article appeared on the scientific dilemma concerning inbreeding wolves in Isle Royale National Park in Lake Superior. In the 1950s, moose crossed an ice bridge from the mainland to populate the island. Soon thereafter, wolves followed the moose. The study of the wolves and moose on Isle Royale has been the subject of more scientific research than any other predator/prey relationship in the world. The island that once did not have wolves and moose is now kept in ecological balance by the presence of the wolf.

The ice bridge that allowed the wolf to freely travel back and forth from the mainland to the island is not forming as it once was because of climate change. It used to form every five years and now it is every 15 years. The avenue has pretty much closed to both moose and wolves. As this was occurring, the wolf populations went from over 50 to just eight. You can already see the problem. Do you bring in more wolves or just let everything collapse?

Not long ago three wolves did cross and things got better, but it didn't take long until the gene pool was again out of kilter. One of those three new wolves became the alpha male, and now every wolf present has his genes. As of April 2014 the park service has decided to not introduce new populations of wolves until more study is done. The final decision is a very important one for NPS, as it could change policy.

Parks Canada also has had some problems keeping with their mission. In 2000, their National Parks Act made "ecological integrity" the number one priority within the country's parks.[32] Of course, "ecological integrity" became a problem for Canadian park wardens. They had to determine just what it means and to try to describe what "natural" really is in their parks.

In the National Park Service, resource management is on an even par with the enjoyment of the visitor. When part of the high country in Yosemite got infested with lodgepole needle miners, the plan was to let nature take its course. Needle miners are a small insect that infest the needles of the lodgepoles to lay their eggs. The next year, the larva will hatch into moths that lay the eggs. It is a two-year cycle. In order for nature to get rid of the insect, very cold winters and heavy snows have to take place at the right time for the snow to knock the needles off the tree and the cold to kill the larva. The lodgepole needle miner is a part of the tree's natural processes, and it is usually present in healthy trees. You need something to happen, like stress from drought, for the tree to get infested. The trees can, however, withstand several years in a row being defoliated without dying.

The National Park Service did intervene when the trees in the campground and Tuolumne Lodge began to die. The "enjoyment for future generations" took priority. A systemic pesticide was used. Years before, the Park Service sprayed large areas by helicopter, not a good management practice since other creatures also were affected. When on horse patrol, I used to take pleasure in telling visitors about how lucky they were to be able to watch forests undergoing change. The dead trees opened the canopy so the sunlight could penetrate and grasses, herbs, and forbs would appear.

---

[32] J.B. MacKinnon, *The Once and Future World, Houghton*, Mifflin, Harcourt, New York, Boston, 2013.

The Challenge of Leadership

Due to all the complex issues, the difficult decisions to be made, and the political environment to navigate, there is nothing secure about being a superintendent of a national park or a state or country park director. A superintendent in a place like Yosemite or Yellowstone is in a politically volatile position. People look over your shoulder all the time. When I first began in this profession, park planners and administrators could make decisions based on what *they* felt was good for the public. There was no such thing as citizen involvement in a master plan process. There is an old saying that good judgment is often the result of experience gained from using bad judgment. There were mistakes made. Park planners and managers were introduced to the fact that there were citizens who were as well versed as they were on environmental and other park-related issues. Now citizen involvement in the planning process is a given. As a private citizen, I have had the opportunity to serve on many county and state park committees and master plan teams along with park professionals and interested and informed citizens. Even with citizen involvement things can be difficult to accomplish.

Yosemite recently completed a Valley Master Plan (VMP) and had most of it approved. Of course, with citizen involvement, there are always several sides of every issue. Congress passed a new Wild and Scenic River Act (WSRA) that almost changed everything in the Valley Master Plan. The Merced River was now a part of that wild river law which required special attention to what activities could take place along the river. The WSRA was written such that some historic vehicle bridges in the Valley had to be removed because they obstructed water flow, and some popular activities had to be eliminated, like horse and bicycle rental.

On one side of the debate were the commercial folks who had use permits to do business in Yosemite and on the other side were the environmentalists. In this case, the National Park Service actually had to deal with three sides because the environmental side was split. On one side were the "realistic environmentalists" and on the other was a small group of people that wanted all commercial and housing development removed from the Valley altogether. When this small group did not get what they wanted, they sued the National Park Service, throwing the whole issue into court and causing the whole process to go back to the drawing board at great cost in time, effort, and labor.

"Not in My Backyard!"

"Not in my backyard" ("nimby") are folks who love parks yet do not want them across the street. Unfortunately, there are plenty of nimbies around for ranger field staff and park administration to handle. People on both sides of a park boundary have to be good neighbors. Even in California, a state that values open space, there are many people who love and enjoy parks as long as they do not bring problems to their everyday lives. They like to see the scenery, but do not like issues a park naturally brings. It is an honest reaction. There are also sections of California as well as other places in this country that do not like government or the land management rules and regulations that government brings. For various reasons there are issues to consider such as environmental and land use regulations, special interests of dog owners, hunters, cyclists, off-road vehicle users, and environmental groups. Politicians and neighborhood organizations often come into play. In some instances, consumption of resources that now becomes preservation is hard for some people to understand. The land is removed from the tax rolls, creating more of a burden for local taxpayers.

Our son, who is a supervisor for California Fish and Wildlife, walked into politics when he became the first manager of a new wildlife area in Northern California almost on the Oregon border. Most ranchers in the area absolutely did not want that wildlife area to happen, citing the demise of "another good ranch." For the most part, they were people who were very anti-government. This was deep seated. Since World War II, the county had wanted to leave the State of California and form, along with other northern counties and counties in Southern Oregon, a new state. Letting them know what was going on instead of keeping them in the dark, giving grazing leases to local ranchers, using local contract people for land leveling and other jobs, getting the local elementary school to raise native plants, giving ranchers credit for adjusting their irrigation schedules so that salmon could come up the Little Shasta River, and spending locally, all served to help with acceptance. The wildlife area gave back much more to the community in dollars than the lost tax base. Although there are still nimbies in the area, for the most part folks have bought in.

When I was at Albright Training Center at the Grand Canyon, creating wilderness was a hot issue. We were reminded by Lon Garrison that it was very difficult to get people in Congress, most of who represent people who live in the inner city, to consider anything like setting aside wilderness or anything natural (like parks). They have more pressing issues, like jobs, poverty, living conditions, and a living wage for the people they represent. Lon also said, and rightly so, that in order to save wilderness (or parks) we need to do something about the issues facing those politicians. Local government representatives also face like issues. Creating a park is not easy.

In fact, the easiest part might be getting the land. Gifts of land for park use are common. In the Southern San Francisco Bay Area of California is Castle Rock State Park that is 100% donated land. The original 26.5 acres were acquired by Dorothy Varian after her husband was killed in an airplane crash in Alaska. Memorial gifts from the employees of Varian Associates and the Sierra Club were added to the purchase. The first land purchase preserved large tafoni (sandstone) rock formations. The park now contains 3600 acres with camping and 32 miles of trails with connections to Big Basin State Park and the ocean. It is a rock climbing mecca for the South Bay.

The twenty-five mile Skyline to the Sea Trail was built in one day by over 2500 volunteers, Boy Scouts, and college students. Our students at West Valley College acted as crew supervisors. After the trail was roughed out, groups adopted sections for maintenance. A special organization coordinates Trail Days that is now a yearly event. Our college at one time maintained a mile section. I also served on the park's

Citizen's Advisory Committee for many years. The park is a labor of love for many people and groups. I am sure there are like stories in other places in California as well as other states.

In January 9, 2014 an article an appeared in the *New York Times* about the difficulty of giving land to the government for a park. Roxanne Quimby owns a large tract of land in northern Maine containing Maine's largest peak, Mount Katahdin, and the endpoint of the Appalachian Trail (which begins in Georgia and is 2200 miles in length). The trail is maintained by 30 trail clubs and managed by the National Park Service and the Appalachian Trail Conservancy. Ms. Quimby's idea is to create a national park on 75,000 acres of pine, spruce, maples and aspen that also contains a large lake. The thought of creating a national park in northern Maine does not sit right with many local residents.

Local tradition in the area is for people to open their private lands to hunting and off-road vehicle use, activities that Ms. Quimby did not embrace. Her land was closed to such use. Anyone who did not allow those activities was looked at with scorn. Closing her lands caused opposition to any ideas she might have regarding national park creation. The locals also envisioned many government regulations and policies about how they used their time. The same arguments appeared about the effect on jobs in the timber industry that were present in the creation of Redwood National Park, California. Timber harvest would be more confined and cut back. New policies would appear, and jobs would disappear. I think that the true reason is that the locals do not want the Federal Government around.

Ms. Quimby finally gave up and gave the land management to her son. He did open 40,000 acres of land to appease the local opposition and suggested setting aside land for a national recreation area adjacent to the new park that would allow hunting and off-road use.

The fly in the ointment is that Ms. Quimby wants the land to be a national park and not just a monument. Parks are created only by an act of Congress. The title "National Park" tends to draw more tourists and thus more money. The proponents need to also sell their representatives to the Federal Government. It will not be an easy task for that to happen. Republicans and Democrats usually vote for such things on strict party lines because they both like to support other Senators and Representatives on their issues so that they get like support on their own. In the end, it will be a problem of convincing people about the economic impact. As usual, it is all about money.

This is not the first time that giving away land has run into difficulty in this country. John D. Rockefeller Jr. spent three decades fighting local opposition to adding land to Grand Teton National Park.[33]

Not all donations are state and federal donations. Some are on the local level. In 2004 a member of a California pioneer family, Walter Cottle Lester, donated a 287-plus acre property in South San Jose to the county and the state for a park. The land has been used for agricultural purposes but is completely surrounded by housing tracts. It is also unique in that Mr. Lester donated the land to two agencies of government. Committees were developed, cooperative agreements made, and the park is under construction (in 2014) and will be managed by the county. Mr. Lester's vision was a park that would save the agricultural heritage of the county once called the "Valley of Heart's Delight." Commercial farming will take place as well as living history programs that will depict what it was like in the early years of the Valley. Great parks are not always natural, and this one was long overdue.

The problem of nimbies can be overcome. Listening, making sure the people's fears are not all realized, and placing them on any advisory or planning task force helps a great deal. Paying attention to public relations is important when confronting political realities.

Political Realities

When our program at West Valley College was in the developmental stage, I sent a listing of the courses we offered to Lemuel (Lon) Garrison, then the Director of the National Park Service's Albright Training

---

[33] Seelye, op. cit.

Center. I had first met Lon when I attended Albright on sabbatical leave. He quickly became my park guru. His answer to the course listing was, "Where is your course on political realities?" I even tried to get the people in Social Sciences to put one together. They tried, but threw up their hands in frustration. It was and is a very complex subject and finding someone to teach it was also difficult. The subject of politics is pretty complex.

Lon was worth listening to when it came to dealing with political issues. He had a lot of practice in his career. When Lon was Superintendent of Yellowstone, he had to deal with several major issues. He placed a curb on development at a time when there was immense pressure to develop more campgrounds. He did it to protect the resources of the park. He restricted the use of motorboats on Yellowstone Lake, which caused him to have pressures brought from governmental as well as private boating concerns.

However, the biggest issue Lon had to confront was the overpopulation of elk, which was causing the decline of the big horn sheep, deer, and beaver. Lon felt that the elk herd had to be reduced in order to adhere to the NPS mandate to leave the park unimpaired. The elk were overgrazing the vegetation. Hunting organizations and state fish and game people from three bordering states applied pressure to allow hunting, and that pressure went as far as Washington, D.C., Lon chose to let the NPS do the thinning, because he felt that there might be demands on other parks in the system, like Yosemite, to allow hunting. In Yellowstone, ranger teams did the hunting, and the teams pruned 4500 elk from the huge herd. The meat was given to Native Americans. There is now new pressure being brought by government to allow hunting in every national park. This legislation is being backed by the National Rifle Association and their friends in Congress.

After seven years at the helm of Yellowstone, Lon was shuttled off to Horace Albright Training Center, where he was able to affect the lives of many national park people in a positive manner, including mine.

Politics will continue to affect park management and field level park employees in such areas as fire and wildlife resource management and recreational activities that are introduced for the benefit of politically-powerful commercial enterprises. Most of those activities and recreational experiences impinge on the reason parks were set aside in the first place. In this modern age, the philosophy and mission that parks are to be managed for future generations seems to be under attack in favor of more "active" sports. In my lifetime, I have already seen backpacking, hang gliding, parachuting, inline skating, sail boarding, competitive rock climbing, free climbing without ropes, off road vehicles and bicycles, snowmobiling, and extreme sports, all affecting park and natural resource management in ways opposite to what the mission of those parks is supposed to be. I have also seen attempts, both locally and in Congress, to change those park mission statements. That has happened recently to the national parks during George W. Bush's administration, when Yellowstone tried to ban snowmobiles in certain sections of the park. It also happened in Santa Clara County, when there was an attempt to change our local county park's mission so that money could be used to build baseball diamonds and soccer fields.

A retired NPS Ranger told me that the politicization of the position and the new guard managers have destroyed the morale, funding, and leadership, and have left a legacy that agrees to the whims of anyone with money to influence management. Managers who stood up for views that did not tie into the political ideology of the party in power often found themselves transferred or, even worse, forced to retire.

With tongue in cheek, I would like to see parks apolitical. Like the Smithsonian is a place to display our national archives, parks are the museums for the natural world, and there should be a desire for them to be thought of that way. Places like the national parks, regional parks, and state parks are storehouses for the natural world. In a utopia, management should be able to reflect professionalism in every way and not be afraid to make decisions that affect resources without any political response that might be career changing. People in the park profession have been transferred or fired over decisions that were political.

I learned early when I was borrowed by the county as a full-time consultant to sit in the director's seat when they found themselves without one. I learned in that position that you can be professionally correct and scientifically correct on a management issue, but political wrong on the same issue. I often felt that some members of the Board of Supervisors could care less about what you know as a professional and felt that "anyone can run a park." The result is that some decisions are to not make a decision. Bill Mott found this to be the case when he first became National Park Service Director. People were "walking on eggshells" because of politics.

When I was at the Albright Training Center during sabbatical leave, the superintendent of Yellowstone National Park told our group that he had to be on a first name basis with the three governors of the states bordering the Park. A recent Yellowstone superintendent was getting complaints from all sides, when he decided to plow the snow off of roads over two weeks later than usual when he was forced by Congress to cut over a million dollars from his park budget. When the park's budget was bare bones to start with, a cut of over 5% really hurt. Local governors and outside commercial interests were crying at the loss of business revenue. Weighing all the issues, like getting rid of seasonal rangers and other public service people, he decided that he would let the sun do it. I personally lost a friend when an avalanche swept him and his bulldozer off the road he was attempting to open early in Yosemite for the commercial interests of those along Highway 395 on the eastern slope of the Sierras. Political pressures caused him to lose his life.

We do know that as long as there is government and people running government, running parks will continue to be a continual educational project for park administrators. Unfortunately, no matter who governs parks, politics will rule.

Chapter 5: The Future of America's Parks

Parks are heading for a huge problem if they want to continue to be what the public desires and wants. On the following pages are some of the problems that I personally foresee as subjects of concern for park rangers and park management. Some of these problems are happening now, and some have already been a concern for many years. Some problems are looming in the future as population grows and society and cultures change.

Funding

Obtaining funding for acquisition, development, and operation of parks has always been a problem. Nathaniel P. Langford, the first person to manage our first national park, Yellowstone, started without a budget to work with, and the financial challenges got worse as people discovered the region. Today America's parks are on the brink of trouble caused by too many people, less available land, and no direction for park and recreation agencies to go. Even if there was a direction for parks to go, there is no money to spend to get there. Lack of available money is probably the biggest problem facing park agencies everywhere, and in a survey I conducted at a recent conference, lack of funding was the number one issue that rangers saw as a future problem. When governmental budgets get tight, money goes to places other than to parks and other agencies that deal with the quality of life. Funds go to fire and police departments and hospitals, services that deal with public safety issues. However, rangers are in parks for public safety too.

Some agencies in the San Francisco Bay Area have their own tax base. They are special districts, created by law. East Bay Regional Parks, Mid-Peninsula Open Space, Sonoma County Open Space, and South County Open Space Authority, and even the Marin County Water District, which allows recreation on their lands, are examples. When land is acquired, managers have to appear.

In the beginning of their agency, one of our local open space districts thought that just purchasing the land and letting it sit would be the way to do things. First named as a regional park district, they even changed that name to "an open space district." As soon as the first parcel was purchased, people were knocking at the door to have them open the parcel to public use. They wanted trails to ride and hike. The district did not do its homework, so did not realize that there were a large number of horse owners close to the boundaries of the open space. Obviously, those people wanted to use it to ride their horses. The district did not want to get into the ranger business, but ended up hiring several rangers because whenever anything is open to the public, things happen. They now own thousands of acres of land patrolled by a very professional ranger unit and maintained by a competent maintenance staff.

The experience of one of our local open space agencies shows that even if you are able to have the money for land, you also need to manage that land. Rangers need to be hired, which points out the necessity of hiring people who can do more than just enforcement. If you do not have the money to buy all the support necessary for maintenance, interpretation, and resource management, then you need someone who can perform at least some of those duties as well as enforce the park rules and regulations.

California also found itself in budget trouble and attempts to sustain a more stable funding for California State Parks failed at the voting booth in 2011, when the Department attempted to attach funding to automobile license fees. It is one of the very few times that park issues have failed at the ballot box. In an effort to find and obtain a more stable and sustainable funding for state parks, California created the Park Stewardship Act (AB 1478) and created a "Parks Forward Commission." Twelve prominent citizens were appointed by the governor to look at the management of state parks and the future needs of parks, and to develop recommendations that will hopefully lead to more financial stability. Other recommendations by this commission can be found in other pages of this book.

In Santa Clara County, the first Director of Parks, Buford "Bob" Amyx, developed a program to enlarge the park system that contained only two parks. He presented a program that would be funded by a bond issue to be repaid by tax revenue. The bond issue to provide Santa Clara County Parks three million dollars was passed by the voters in 1959.[34] However, Bob thought that they needed a more stable method of funding the Department. An amendment to the County Charter would create a pool of money for parks. It was not an easy sell, but through the efforts of many people, the Charter Amendment passed.

At first, the money was set aside at a rate of 10 cents per $100 assessed property value. That first amendment was not a permanent one, and it has been renewed several times since inception. The last time it was passed by a whopping 82% of the voters! The 10 cents has been much reduced, but the fund has still created millions of dollars. The county soon became land rich but operations poor. Another trip to the voting booth allowed the department to use some of that fund for operations. The county is very lucky to have had such visionary proponents for parks in the early years.

There are many advocates for parks in the area where I live. Parks or open space could not survive without their support. The effort made to pass the Park Charter Amendment is a prime example of local citizens banding together to support the parks.

It seems that interpretive functions of parks are often the first things to be cut when budget time rolls around. These educational functions like guided walks, nature walks and talks, visitor center information stations, and visits to local schools, should be considered critical to park management. An educated park public is necessary if parks are to survive in the future. Children who visit parks will soon be old enough to vote. Well-supported interpretive functions can ease park management problems, as well. Park foundations and associations, like the Yosemite Conservancy, the California State Park Foundation,

---

[34] David Weintraub, "History of Santa Clara County Parks," an unpublished document, 2011.

and other supporting foundations for parks, provide much-needed political support when that budget crunch appears. The interpretive function will become an important issue since future park employees might have "nature deficit disorder."

What happens when emergencies happen that shrink an already no-meat-on-the-bones budget? Searches happen. Rescues happen, and fires are sometimes started, either by nature or humans. Nature will strike back at you at times. One February in the early 1980s, we had 19 inches of rain in 36 hours in the Santa Cruz Mountains. Campground roads, water systems in parks, and road and trail bridges spanning streams were washed away. Some park agencies put funds aside to prepare for such events. Some do not. Some budget for events like searches and if the event takes more money to complete and the agency is stuck with the consequences and must make decisions about what to do.

A great story about what might happen in a search is found in Bruce Bytnar's book entitled *A Park Ranger's Life*. The chapter on a long search for a lost National Park Service employee in a muddled jurisdiction that had several agencies involved shows just what could happen when it came to costs. The local sheriff, who had the responsibility for conducting the search, did not have the training or the funds to conduct it. The Forest Service got involved with the search and the Park Service was not very supportive. In the end, the Park Service got stuck with most of the bill, which was around $500,000 dollars![35]

Parks will have to begin to look at other sources of revenue. We will see more funds coming from supporting foundations and perhaps even the possibility of turning parks over to private enterprise. That is already happening or being suggested by some. The Yosemite Conservancy provides millions of dollars for resource management and maintenance projects in the Park. You can even purchase a California license plate with Yosemite's Half Dome on it. The money from the

---

[35] Bruce W. Bytmar, *A Park Ranger's Life, Thirty Two Years Protecting Our National Parks*, Wheatmark, Tucson, Arizona, 2010.

license plates goes to the Conservancy. Several associations in California support state parks locally. They will become more important as the years go by. Foundations are very important in funding science, interpretation, and resource management, as well as for garnering public support on important political issues.

Recently a commission to study California State Parks asked that government look hard at which state park services could be turned over to private interests or to county or regional park systems. They also suggested that the department find different ways to create more revenue.[36]

We probably will see park agencies share the responsibility of some of their lands. Like what has happened in Arizona, state park land might be "loaned" to an adjacent city or county for management. We have one park in Santa Clara County where land purchase and planning was shared with state parks and another park was "loaned" to an adjacent land management agency for management.

Private Enterprise

Giving parks to private enterprise to manage has its pluses and minuses. On the plus side, the rangers would only have to worry about law enforcement because private companies would have no enforcement jurisdiction. Restroom and other facility maintenance and the equipment and supplies to do it would no longer be the responsibility of the agency. The government would not have to purchase and maintain lawn mowers, as an example, or hire and fire maintenance employees or provide them fringe benefits. Agencies usually can get rid of a private company if they are not doing the job. Sometimes getting rid of a public employee is such a long drawn-out process that it isn't worth the effort even to try.

On the minus side, there is a certain pride in ownership. Private and commercial operations are driven by dollars. Public agencies are service oriented. Wearing a park agencies uniform means something.

---

[36] "Hoover Commission Executive Summary," 2013.

You still have to provide law enforcement authority and probably manage the natural resources. Law enforcement is more costly than maintenance people in terms of hourly wages. Private enterprise in parks does need supervision, and that costs money. You just cannot give a park to a company and walk away.

Although we now have excellent volunteer or paid docents giving interpretive programs, rangers are always better because they represent the park agency and because of the image they bring. It is the image of what the public perceives a ranger to be.

Parks are mostly seasonal, and it is hard for a private concern to make enough money in the few months that visitors are present. In order to make sure they earn a profit, prices are sometimes high.

After long years of a failure to address funding problems, it got down to where California was thinking about closing 70 parks. When individuals and foundations came to the forefront to keep that from happening, it was discovered that State Parks had somehow hidden $54 million in two separate accounts. That caused a huge lack of trust in the Department of Parks and Recreation and how it was being run, as well as funded. The Director of California State Parks put together a coalition of 13 private businesses, education, and non-profit people to help revamp the system, make it more financially sound, and look at potential revenue sources. These experts were to tell him how to best run state parks and generate revenue. The attitude this encourages then becomes one of consumption rather than preservation. Parks are not created to make money or be commercial.

A very successful company, California Land Management (CLM), began in 1981 when they signed a contract to run a local park in Sunnyvale, California. They have since expanded to include several companies that manage campgrounds as well as park maintenance, interpretation services, and resource management throughout the western states. Most of their campgrounds are with the United States Forest Service. It could be that their services might expand into other parks and agencies because of government funding problems.

When I taught at West Valley College, we ran three campgrounds for the United States Forest Service (USFS) in the summer. They were located in Sierra National Forest. It was a pilot program to see if campgrounds could be operated by private enterprise, because the USFS was having a problem running them due to lack of funding. West Valley ran them for several years at a profit. The campgrounds provided educational experiences during the school year, including preparing budgets and the planning and construction of moveable structures like entrance stations that we could not leave there during the winter. Operating the campgrounds put $100,000 into the college coffers over ten years, as well as provided summer employment for students! It was a great cooperative venture that ended when I retired. The campground venture also supported other projects on the college campus. We bought equipment for our supporting biology classes, purchased the most modern interpretive equipment, gave funding to the library for park management periodicals and books, and bought three pickup trucks, tools, and equipment for our school year involvement at Sanborn County Park. The visiting public enjoyed their stays, the clean restrooms and campsites, and the fact that our people were always on site to serve their needs.

However, having an institution like a college run something like a campground is a lot different than someone trying to make a living at doing it. It was ideal for our program as it occurred in the summer and the support given by the college was huge. For example, the college just extended their campus to include the campgrounds, thus covering the facilities with liability insurance. The funds the college provided were needed to begin the enterprise so that salaries could be paid until the program could afford to pay them out of revenue. Chico State University Foundation also operates a very successful campground operation for the Forest Service that has placed over a million dollars into the coffers of the foundation.

Resource Management

I read a book entitled *The End of Oil*, by Paul Roberts, which was an eye opener. It was published in 2005 and some things have changed since then. We have already reached the red line of 450 ppm CO_2 predicted for 2020 by the author. It made me think that another of the problems parks and open spaces are going to face in the future is that energy is found below the surface in some of that protected ground. Already the search for thermal energy has threatened Old Faithful and other geyser fields in Yellowstone National Park. Drilling for thermal energy has already affected the geysers in Iceland. No one can predict whether drilling for thermal energy, even outside of Yellowstone, could affect the geyser basins inside the park.

Oil is certainly found below some of the protected land in Alaska and maybe other places. I remember a helicopter crashing in Yosemite when a government scientific crew was taking soundings for oil exploration. The oil fields of the world that are easily found have been found already, and lands that have been off limits to drilling may be forced to open. The oil interests have powerful political lobbies.

The Wilderness Society has stated that the drive to drill for oil is sending gas development deeper into our wild places and our most beloved lands. Places like Arches National Park in Utah, Dinosaur National Monument in Colorado, and Chaco Canyon in New Mexico are being threatened. The Society states that these places, among others in the West, directly provide six million jobs connected to outdoor recreation and over $600 billion to the economy annually.[37]

Managing a park's natural resources is going to be more challenging in the future. Encroachment by commercial and residential growth is already happening, mostly in regional, county, and urban regional parks, but also in some national and state parks. The "Parks Forward" Commission in California recommended that all parks agencies get together to maintain sustainable open space. In a recent email to me, a former state park ranger pointed out to me that Frederick Law

---

[37] Wilderness Society mailer, October 2013.

Olmsted Sr. hit the nail on the head when he said in his report to the Yosemite Grant Commission in 1864 that there will forever be a conflict in providing recreational opportunities to the public.[38]

Information on how ecosystems function is changing almost daily. Few park agencies outside the National Park Service or Forest Service have budgets for science. Consequently, little research has been done to assist urban, county, and regional park systems on park use. The need for that science has never been greater, and local colleges and universities need to be necessary partners with park agencies everywhere. The science of managing the resources contained in our parks is changing rapidly and most field personnel are not tuned to the science, nor is there funding available to train or to hire someone who is. Local colleges can help here, as well.

Invasive vegetative species will continue to be a problem. Lackluster interest by some folks in management, lack of expertise by field personnel in smaller park systems in particular, and the lack of funding to hire that expertise and underwrite projects will be the norm. Right now some issues are bottomless and throwing money at them is like pounding sand into a rat hole. As long as birds fly, horses that do not use weed-free hay use trails, and there are neighbors that do not care, we will never get a handle on this issue. The USFS requires weed-free hay, as do some national parks and state parks. Although it would be extremely hard to enforce, it is time every agency has that policy. There will need to be an effort to go beyond park boundaries to the land owners that abut the park boundaries. Getting rid of invasive species has to become a cooperative effort between public and private lands, since it makes little sense to do it on one side of the fence and not the other.

The Leopold Report

In 1963 A. Starker Leopold, the son of Aldo Leopold, wrote a report to the National Park Service that served as a guide on wildlife manage-

---

[38] Miles Standish, email to the author, May 22, 2013.

ment in the national parks. The Leopold Report "stated that parks should be managed to the illusion prior to the entrance of European man." A lot of park agencies beside the National Park Service bought into that report, even though no one really knew what that was. I must admit that it was a concept that I taught to students at West Valley College. As the years went by, I started to change my tune a little because people were beginning to talk about not knowing what that illusion really is. Recently, the report has been revisited. The goal now is to "steward NPS resources for continuous change that is not yet fully understood," and also, "to provide visitors with transformative experiences." The Coalition to Protect America's National Parks, formerly the Coalition of National Park Service Retirees, an organization of former administrators, rangers, and other employees of NPS, called this last statement confusing.[39] The science of resource management needs funding and backing in all agencies. Interpretive services by naturalists will need to be enhanced and not cut back, if that is what they are talking about. The public will need a new vision as to what is going on when they enter a park and see forests of trees under stress or dying and wildlife no longer present because of climate change.

Climate and Environmental Challenges

Park management is facing management challenges that they can do little about except to make an effort to educate visitors about environmental issues. Things outside the park boundaries that management has no control over are affecting, and will continue to affect, resources inside the park even more than they are now.

Air Quality

Smog has already affected trees in the L.A. Basin and elsewhere in this country. Viewsheds are already being affected by bad air. In the Great Smoky Mountains, visibility years ago used to be almost a hun-

---

[39] Maureen Finnerty, "Comments on Revisiting Leopold," letter written to National Park Service Director Jonathan Jarvis, January 22, 2013.

dred miles on a clear day. That figure has been cut to 40 miles. Some days in the Grand Canyon, smog from L.A. and nearby power plants fills the canyon so you cannot see the river from the canyon rim. The bottom of the Canyon is no longer the bastion for clean air it once was. Smog occurs on warm days in the Santa Clara Valley where it affects the viewshed when seen from high places in our parks.

Climate and Ecosystem Changes

The Rocky Mountain Climate Organization made a prediction in October 2010 that California's parks will be in some peril because of temperature change. Some of the parks will see a temperature change of not less than +6 °F, or more than +8 °F by the year 2070. Creatures are already changing migratory habits, and drought and other climate swings are becoming more common. Muir Woods National Monument in California will have a temperature similar to what San Diego historically has. These kinds of shifts will affect both flora and the fauna of any park. I read in *Audubon Magazine* some years ago that the American Goldfinch, the State Bird of New Jersey, soon would not be found there. Some mammals like the Pica, a small rodent found in the Sierra Mountains, are now found at higher altitudes than before. The Mexican Grackle, a crow-like bird, is now found in abundance in Phoenix, Arizona, when just a few years ago they were not present at all. Some visitor center displays may have to focus on what used to be there. Someone who does not believe in climate change needs to be more observant and let nature tell them that it is happening. Good rangers should be able to interpret and educate the public on changing environments.

Drought caused by climate change is also going to be a future forest and grassland management issue that field rangers and park managers have to face.

According to climate scientists, sea levels are going to rise. Predicting how that affects coastal park units within the National Park Service is a complex issue, mainly because not only do the oceans rise, but scientists are discovering that the loss of something like a glacier might cause the land to recede or sink. Coastal beaches and marshes in national parks, state, county, and urban parks certainly will be affected by a rise in sea level. New studies were begun in 2013 by national park scientists and cooperative scientists to study what storm surges and sea rise might do to coastal parks, citing that over 100 national parks are vulnerable to those combined effects. The national park service findings and all their research about sea rise will need to be shared with the coastal state and local park systems, since few states, if any, have research budgets. [40]

Fire as a Management Tool

One of the problems in managing park resources is the use of fire as a management tool. In our county, as well as other park systems throughout the United States, forests and park lands have been protected from fire for many years and are getting less and less healthy. We now know that fire is an important part of the health of the forest ecosystem. I once asked Dr. Jan Van Wagtendonk, a United States Geological Survey scientist, whether all native vegetation was connected to fire. He thought that might be the case.

Forestry professionals will tell you that a healthy forest is a diverse forest, and many of the trees present in our parks are mature, some at the end of their lifespans. Pictures from the past show how open the forests used to be when fire was a part of the natural scene. As John Muir once said, "you could ride a horse through the forests of Yosemite." You would have a great deal of trouble doing that today. Because of the absence of fire, huge amounts of forest litter are present, as are ladder fuels. Ladder fuels are small trees and brush that would allow a fire to reach into the higher branches of the trees. When a fire tops out in the larger trees, a crown fire is created and fire storms are a result. Litter and ladder fuels rule out the re-introduction of fire because it would be too dangerous. The fuel load is too great.

---

[40] Maria Caffery and Rebecca Beavers, "Planning for the impact of sea-level rise on U.S. National Parks," *Park Science*, Summer 2013, Volume 30, Number 1.

Dr. Thomas Harvey, former Professor at San Jose State University (now deceased) and an expert on fire in the redwood ecosystem, once told me that if a fire ever started in the Santa Cruz Mountains in California, firefighters would not have much of a chance of putting it out for quite a while. Also, it is not a case of *whether* it will happen, but *when*.

The best way to lessen the chances of a huge fire event would be to remove the litter and ladder fuels via hand labor and that is almost cost prohibitive. Grassland problems can be controlled by grazing. Some park forests may have to be mechanically thinned, which could lead to timber harvests. The harvesting of timber in a park would be a huge political problem. Park rangers and administrators would have the monumental task of educating park visitors and environmental groups like the Sierra Club.

Experts will also tell you that there certainly is a risk in using fire as a management tool. "Prescriptions" are sometimes used that try to eliminate the risks. In Yosemite, if a fire starts above 8000 feet elevation, then it is allowed to burn. Of course, if the fire threatens developed property, it is put out. Expert fire ecologists take into consideration temperature of the air, wind speed, fuel load and fuel moisture, control of the smoke plume, and fuel breaks, both natural and created, before resource managers light the match. Even though the burn is within the scientific parameters, if there is a change in temperature, a wind shift, or a fire jumping a fire line, that can evoke the dangers associated with prescribed burns. Prescribed burns are always a risk because situations can change without warning.

The "let-burn" policy became a subject of great controversy during and after the Yellowstone fires of 1988. The Yellowstone Fire started by lightning in several different places that joined together into one huge fire that burned for several months. The fire became the largest wildfire ever recorded in the United States. The fire began in a let-burn area inside of the park and also in a forest outside the park. Almost 800,000 acres of the park were affected and the suppression cost over $120 million. Eventually over 9000 firefighters (including park rangers from other parks) were assigned to fight the fire, along with

4000 military personnel. It burned well into September, when Mother Nature put it out with a snowstorm. My family had visited in Yellowstone several years prior to the fire, and I had been astonished when I saw the fuel load in the lodgepole forests. Downed trees were everywhere. I thought then that it was ripe for a fire and was a disaster about to happen.

At the fire's onset, the biggest pressure to extinguish it was from the surrounding gateway communities that depended on the park for their livelihood. It was costing them dearly in lost revenue from tourism. Politicians and the media jumped on the bandwagon and began having second thoughts about the service's policies concerning fire. The fire, according to the media, was destroying Yellowstone.

Bill Mott, then Director of the National Park Service, was busy trying to put out fires of his own. He spent a great deal of time defending the fire policies of his service and, I am sure, defending his job as Director. Eventually the Yellowstone fire affected fire programs everywhere in the Park Service. All use of fire, in whatever manner, was placed on hold. I had the chance to be in a burned area just outside of the park a few years afterward and discovered that the area had recovered handsomely. In fact, the fire was probably the best thing that ever happened to Yellowstone. New lodgepole pines were sprouting and wildflowers were bountiful.

The problem of the control and use of fire has put park administrators in a huge "Catch-22" political situation. Politicians represent the voting public and those who live on the borders of parks know the risk of fire. Despite the science, politicians are not happy about letting a fire start on purpose, regardless of how it betters the park environment. The use of prescribed fire is also a problem with some park administrators, as their jobs sometimes are on the line if they use it.

In early August 2013 a huge forest fire that appeared to be a human caused broke out in the mountains near Yosemite National Park. The fire burned over 250,000 acres and cost over $127 million to contain, not including the cost to repair the environmental damage and the losses suffered by the economies of nearby towns.[41] As mentioned previously, summer is the most important time for gateway communities to make up for their yearly expenses. It was the time people visited Yosemite and the other mountain open space attractions and the cost to the economy was in the millions of dollars at a time when the communities were still recovering from a recession.

The Urbanization of America

Habitat Encroachment

Almost all parks have political boundaries rather than ecological ones. The boundaries were created by governmental action. Due to population growth, people are living right up to the natural edges of parks. That kind of encroachment has even hit the outskirts of our national parks. People are retiring to the borders of parks, liking the fact that they are so near to nature in its best forms. Yosemite gateway cities like Mariposa and Oakhurst are communities that depend upon Yosemite and the resulting tourism for most of their livelihood. Gatlinburg, Tennessee, a gateway to Great Smoky National Park, has become an attraction in its own right. Carnivals, helicopter rides, and arcades are everywhere. One might say that sleazy trappings abound, and there are far more hotel beds in the town than there are people in the town's population. It has become a target destination for people. Not Great Smoky Mountain Park, but Gatlinburg! Leaving the serenity of that great park, Gatlinburg hits you right in the face.

I team-taught a course at San Jose State University on the effects of recreation on the environment to a group of hospitality majors, people who will run hotels and restaurants. They thought Gatlinburg was "neat." Some of our most historic areas, like Gettysburg Battle Field and Manassas Battlefield, both pivotal Civil War sites, are completely surrounded by development and are under constant pressure from outside development interests.

---

[41] *Rim Fire Near Yosemite Fully Contained After More Than 2 Months* San Francisco Chronicle, 10/25/2013

In Santa Clara County, California, there are several parks that used to be out in the "boonies" and are now surrounded by increasing human densities. Homes encircle some of those parks on all sides.

The picture below is an example of a park in California's Santa Clara County with development right up to the boundary of the park. Most parks in that system are seeing boundaries shared by development. Just as parks have to be good neighbors, those people whose boundaries are next to public land also have to be good neighbors. Some people do not like parks in their backyards, usually because parks bring with them an increase in vehicle and foot traffic. Unfortunately, there are plenty of nimbies around for ranger field staff and park administration to handle.

Harvey Bear Ranch County Park in
Santa Clara County, California.
(Photo by Donald Rocha)

There also could be an increase in crime and vandalism in the parks. My experience as a ranger has shown me that locals can be a problem, even at a remote natural park. Encroachment creates an increase in automotive traffic and the problems it causes. Automobiles cause animal mortality and add to the smog levels. There will also be an increase in non-native and invasive plants. Most park agencies I know are already battling this problem, and quite frankly, it is a never-ending task. In some cases, there will be no turnaround.

There are several problems for park management caused by development bordering park boundaries. There is an increase in feral dog and cat populations and the associated problems. Cats, both feral and domestic, prey on songbirds so much that it is the species' major cause of death. Cats kill an estimated 1.7 billion birds a year in this country.

Studies have shown that light pollution from the homes and businesses has an adverse effect on wildlife.[42] Light might confuse and cause dispersal problems. Wildlife, like feral pigs, coyotes, and mountain lions, will start appearing in neighborhood backyards.

In a sense, most regional parks will soon become urban parks and will have the same problems. Neighbors who enjoy the view will not be happy when mountain lions appear in their backyards and the deer eat their formal landscaping.

Wildlife Management

How wildlife is managed is a very large political issue in this country. On one side are the environmentalists and on the other are the ranchers and the farmers and the outdoorsmen. Each side has political clout. Each side wants wildlife to flourish but for different reasons. Parks are sanctuaries for wildlife where they are usually protected from being harvested, although there are some protected places in Alaska still open to hunting. Visitors come to parks to view wildlife.

Unfortunately wildlife cannot read signs and often go beyond the park boundaries. When I was a wilderness ranger in Yosemite, hunters lined up just outside the boundaries during deer season to shoot deer when they wandered off the reservation. The same thing happens in Yellowstone during elk season. Hunters want healthy elk

---

[42] *Stewardship Across Boundaries,* Edited by Richard Knight, and Peter Landres, Island Press, Washington, D.C., p. 178.

populations to fill their freezers. I know several park rangers who are avid elk hunters.

The politics of elk population in Yellowstone continues to be a huge problem even today. Instead of thinning the park population of elk by hunting, as was the case during Garrison's career, the National Park Service and the Fish and Wildlife Service lobbied government to successfully re-introduce the gray wolf into the Yellowstone ecosystem. The result of the wolf being present has been a huge positive in changing the way the Yellowstone ecosystem functions. Not only were elk numbers reduced (50%), but because wolves kept the elk moving around, that ended their habit of frequenting the meadows to browse on the willows that the beavers depended upon for their existence. After the wolf re-introduction, the willows again flourished and the beaver population has rebounded in large numbers. The dams that they build are a benefit to many species of wildlife. Birds and fish have returned in large numbers. After the wolf was extirpated in 1926, the coyote numbers increased as the elk population exploded. The numbers of coyotes has now diminished. Coyotes preyed on smaller mammals and seldom went after elk. Their absence has helped the fox, the beaver, and other small critters.

Wildlife scientists and park rangers find what is happening exciting. It is not often that they get an opportunity to study a whole ecosystem undergoing change. Ranchers don't appreciate the results as much. Ranchers continue to work politically to eliminate the wolf completely. Deals were made from the beginning to compensate ranchers for any losses attributed to wolves. A fund was set up by the Defenders of Wildlife, a private organization, which has paid ranchers over $1.4 million in compensation for cattle losses as a result of being preyed upon by wolves. The political process has taken many years. The idea began in 1974, and the results are still a political football to be kicked around. It took until 1995 to get through the politics to get the job done. There is a healthy number of wolves now present in Yellowstone. From an original total of 66, the wolf has increased to 325.

Of course every move is scrutinized by both sides of the issue. As late as 2013, lawsuits are still pending as to who has authority for the management of wolves. For the common park visitor, seeing a wolf is now the most anticipated visual experience, and for some, the very reason they come to Yellowstone, and they bring their checkbooks and cash that add to the local economy.

Other introductions of wolves have happened in New Mexico and Arizona. In New Mexico, five of the last known Mexican gray wolves were captured and a breeding program begun. Now there are over 300, with a goal to put them back into their original habitat. Red wolves were introduced into Great Smoky Mountains National Park in the early 1990s. That program was canceled when the population died back from disease, lack of food, and because they had trouble staying within the park boundaries.

California's Santa Clara Valley was once teeming with elk and pronghorn before Europeans settled there. Because they were traditionally a part of the ecosystem, elk and pronghorn were reintroduced into one of our local county parks several years ago. That original elk herd has since became three herds and is beginning to become more visible. I fully expect elk to become a pest to local landowners very soon. One of our local golf courses is already experiencing damage. Our son, a manager for the California Department of Fish and Wildlife once told me, "Dad, an elk goes where an elk wants to."

I have been told that hunting elk in our local Mount Diablo Range is more of a money maker for ranchers than raising cattle. Although the freeways act as a barrier, there are plenty of places where they can cross over and populate the other side. It is only a matter of time until they migrate into other open space areas in the County. It will not be long until they become a political issue as well.

Right now the pronghorns are behaving themselves.

Most wildlife move across the park boundary to migrate or to pass their genes on to other generations. Their habitat has been fragmented and wildlife will be adversely affected genetically unless corridors are created for them to move from one place to another. One park in the San Francisco Bay Area has already seen some of that happening. Ardenwood Farm Regional Park, in the East Bay, found itself surrounded by development. The deer had to be trapped and relocated because of problems caused by inbreeding and starvation.

Park Sustainability

The increase in human population could put more pressure on the existing park systems in this country and that would cause management to begin to reconsider the unpopular decision to create carrying capacities in parks. Politicians do not like to hear those words, mostly because they are the ones who feel the pressure from park users. As rangers like to put it, our parks are beginning to be loved to death. As someone once told me, "You don't continue to sell 1000 tickets to a rock concert in an auditorium that holds 600 without having some damage."

Putting too many people in a park will cause damage to resources. Wildlife will have difficulty surviving and there will be more wildlife/human interaction. It will be up to the people with their feet on the ground, the park rangers, to come up with ways to manage people.

Reservations and higher entrance fees can be used to control park access. The collection of entrance fees in one of our local parks eliminated "cruising the scene" by local teens looking for action. The entrance stations are now only manned when use is high because of the cost to collect the money. One year in Yosemite, we lost thousands of dollars in entrance fees because we did not have the funds to hire anyone to collect them.

We now have reservations for camping in our parks. Perhaps someday a visitor may have to get a reservation just to visit some parks. Trying to sell the value of preservation is going to take time and effort to convince the new urban society that capacity issues are important to saving land for future generations.

An article in the San Francisco Chronicle (September 17, 2013) stated that the National Park Service is considering placing a reservation system into place for a parking space at Muir Woods National Monument. The monument is experiencing over 6000 people per day on weekends, which caused park planner Brian Aviles to state that there was no way that the Park Service could provide a good visitor experience when there were that many people. Parking lots are full every weekend, with people cruising around waiting for a space to open, or parking alongside a narrow road leading to the park's entrance and walking into the monument. Some have to walk over a mile or so.

A reservation system for parking is in essence creating a carrying capacity for the facility. Creating parking spaces in order to control visitation is not a new concept, but a reservation system certainly is. There appears to be no acceptable alternative. Land is not available to create new parking except land owned by the National Park Service outside the monument and much further away. A weekend bus service has been in place from Highway 101 in Marin County and has been very successful. However, the bus service only runs from May to October.

Of course the use of buses to move people to and throughout parks is not a new concept. Buses are used in Grand Canyon, Yosemite, Harper's Ferry, and California State Parks' Hearst Castle, to name a few. Lessoning the impacts of too many cars in parks is becoming more and more popular. Yosemite has had that in place for many years. I recently visited Yosemite for five days, parked my vehicle, and never got back into it until I got in it to go home. I never missed it!

Electronic Encroachment

People who like to camp, hike, and use the outdoors usually do so because they like to "get away from it all" and enjoy doing things they could not do in the city. They enjoy getting away from the hustle and bustle of modern society and enjoy being in a primitive environment.

When I was a scoutmaster in the 1970s, our troop spent one weekend a month camping in one of our local parks. In order to get them to try to enjoy their surroundings, we had one basic rule. We never brought activities or things with us that we can use or do at home. No Frisbees, no footballs, no radios or other electronic devices, and no playing cards. The scouts never seemed to miss these things. I wanted the guys to enjoy nature, so we did only those things that we could do in a park environment.

Today with more portable electronic devices, people don't want to be away from their modern communication conveniences. Everyone seems to have a cell phone or an iPod® and they seem to be in constant communication with others. Telephones can now ring in the site next to yours at any hour, and the sound of electronic games pierces the silence of the campground. Rangers complain that their offices are now being called by people on cell phones for every little thing that happens, like a bear sighting a hundred yards away.

There is some defense for cell phone use when a person is lost or injured. Cell phone calls can be traced, making it easier to locate a lost or injured person. Cell phones can be educational as well. The Audubon Society now offers apps for cell phones that identify birds, complete with the sounds of their songs.

Just recently the city of San Francisco announced that, thanks to a Silicon Valley company, their citizens can now enjoy having Wi-Fi in all their parks. The announcement was followed by an editorial telling us "old timers" that things were not going to change because "nature, flowers, and other things" will still be there. I guess they do not know about correcting the problems of nature deficit disorder.

Unmanned Aircraft

Unmanned aircraft (drones) first appeared in the wars in the Middle East. Obviously used for military purposes and carrying rockets, cameras, and GPS units, they can search out and destroy the enemy in very accurate fashion. In fact, the United States Air Force is training more drone operators than pilots. The size of the military drone is like that of a small airplane. Technology has now taken the drone to a size of a model airplane and even as small as a hummingbird. It is becoming an industry in the billions of dollars.

This new technology has led law enforcement to jump upon the use of drones as a preventive device or to track felons and other criminals and to provide officer safety.

It certainly will not be long until park management can also see the advantages of using these devices. Vancouver Canada is now using them to harass geese in an effort to get them to migrate away from public parks. As a former Yosemite park ranger that has been on many searches and rescues of people in my career, I can see where drones could be a huge help in conducting flights during searches. Fitted with television cameras and, perhaps infrared cameras that can detect heat, they sure would be a lot cheaper than a helicopter. Drones could check rock and mountain climbing routes and the condition of accident victims up close. Drones are very easy to operate. All you would need is a smart phone and the drone and can be carried in the trunk of your patrol car. Certainly park rangers could also use them in their enforcement duties just as urban police officers. Sure would be nice to be able to look behind that tree.

Drones can also be applied to tracing collared wildlife, as well as hundreds of other resource management uses. It is certainly a cheap way to inventory natural resources. Even landscape architects could use such a device when planning for a new park. The park management uses are almost endless. With funding a problem everywhere, an investment in this technology could be a god-send.

Of course with all this hanging on the horizon, citizens are beginning to show their concern. No one takes their freedom more seriously than an American, and privacy has become a real issue when drones can be hovering over your backyard, looking into your windows, or disrupting the silence of your park stay. The last one is already beginning to be a concern in our national parks. Drones are appearing in likes of the Grand Canyon, Yosemite, and other Western parks. Those parks are starting to ban their use. It appears that will soon be a concern in all park agencies.

As I have mentioned in this book, park management has faced all kinds of challenges. Like any new piece of recreational equipment, it all depends upon who is using it. Horses and off-road bike riders can cause impact or be responsible. It all depends upon who is riding.

Although modern communication devices are not a threat to managing park resources, they are a threat to the sanctity of why we have parks and our reasons for being there.

Changing Population

I had an email exchange with retired California State Park Ranger Jeff Price recently about where California State Parks sent their cadets after their initial training. I had always thought that they were sent to the beaches because the enforcement was more intense there and it was an enforcement hardening procedure. Jeff told me that in the '60s and '70s most openings were at the beaches, and cadets were sent where the openings were, not specifically for the law enforcement experience. The reason there were openings was that the rangers working at that time transferred out of the beaches to more tranquil and sedate places in the park system as quickly as they were able to do so. Now the new rangers are most likely to have to go to those sedate and tranquil places because that is now where the openings are. New state park cadets are now more tuned to being in urban areas where the action is, where the environment is more "civilized," and they are more uncomfortable in a rural setting than an urban one.[43]

The demographics of America are changing. More than 80% percent of America's population is now urban, and that population has increased 12.1% between the years 2000 and 2010 compared to 9.7% for the nation as a whole. To qualify as an urbanized area according to the Census Bureau, an area must encompass at least 50,000 people within the city and the "urban fringe," or 1000 people per square mile. The result is that cities and towns are spreading out further from their original limits, and homes are beginning to abut the fence lines of county, regional, and state parks, as well as some national parks.

---

[43] Jeff Price, email correspondence with author, March 2013.

The country's population is aging and park visits are increasing in non-summer months. Some school districts have year-long school, causing family vacations at times other than just the summer months. Visitation patterns will change, if they have not already. That struck me as abundantly clear, when I could not find a parking space in Yosemite Valley on a weekend in October 2011. It has also become abundantly clear as people grow older, facilities that can be used by this age group lessen. I recently gave a talk to a "Golden Age" group of people at a nearby facility. When one asked me where he could go on a nature hike that was an easy walk, I had trouble answering him. That was an eye opener. These are the people who vote.

The National Park Service has found that the ages of park visitors have gone through change as well. The number of people over 64 who have visited Great Smoky Mountains National Park has risen seven percent since 1996. At the same time, the number of visitors under fifteen has fallen four percent.

There is a concern in the National Park Service that the new populations of people coming to America from other countries could be a huge problem. Most are coming from places that have no history of parks and have no cultural connections to places like Yosemite, or the Everglades. People who have had free rein to hunt in open spaces think that our park lands are also open for that activity, which is causing some minor poaching situations.

Finding New Rangers

An urbanized America will be providing our new rangers and park managers. If Richard Louv's statement in *"Last Child in the Woods"* is correct, and young children are starting to have "nature deficit disorder," the demographics will be such that we will have park administrators and field personnel who are more tuned to urban than rural environments, having lost touch with nature and natural environments. The future of our parks and the profession of the park ranger will be in those hands.

The Park Management Program at West Valley College that had been a huge part of my life since 1970 is now under pressure to put more students in the classroom. The problem is that there don't seem to be enough interested potential students. That issue is becoming abundantly clear when you look at the enrollments in colleges and universities that offer a park management program. All seem to be suffering. It is a time when programs like West Valley's are of utmost importance. It is time to champion a career in parks.

Are Parks for Everyone?

Obviously park visitors come in all sizes and shapes and all ages. However, I do not believe that the "typical" park visitor represents society in a true sense. There is a definite need to make parks more attractive to minority cultures. Yosemite, as well as most parks, is still pretty much middle and upper middle class, white America. A 2011 survey showed that Hispanics accounted for fewer than 10% of American park visitors and African Americans made up just 7%. Asian Americans made up 3% and Native Americans were at 1%. Research has shown that the "typical" national park visitor is more than likely a person who is a college graduate and even has graduate degrees. As an example, I once read a research paper that determined that 80% of the people that attended interpretive programs had at least two years of college.

Hope for the Future

The times ahead for parks are filled with great uncertainty because of the challenges mentioned in this chapter. Unfortunately there are no silver bullet answers. There have been challenges in the past as well. Fortunately there have been many people who have cared about the parks and who have stepped up to the challenge.

Chapter 6: People Who Have Made a Difference

Most of us are hero worshipers. Like any kid, I had major league baseball heroes, and heroes on the local high school basketball team. As we grow older, our values change. Athletes are pushed aside to make room for more important persons.

In my classroom at West Valley College, in the space between the blackboard and the ceiling of the room, I put a row of pictures of people considered to be heroes of the outdoors: John Muir, Aldo Leopold, Steven Mather, Rachel Carson, Teddy Roosevelt, and Frederick Law Olmsted. They certainly were not, nor had they ever been, park rangers. However, what they did to support what rangers vow to protect was monumental. Anyone interested in the outdoors, in conservation and preservation, and in environmental issues would know who those people were and what they had meant to the outdoor recreation movement in America. By displaying those pictures, we hoped that students would remember that those kinds of people made a huge contribution to their profession and we thought students ought to know who they were. We have already mentioned Olmsted in this book. In case there are people out there who do not know, here are some of the things the others contributed.

Early Heroes and Heroines

John Muir

There are many books written about John Muir. Revered by people who love Yosemite and the national parks, this man who was born in Scotland and raised in Wisconsin did more than any other person to bring the glories of Yosemite National Park into the national limelight by the books that he wrote and the articles that he contributed to newspapers, magazines and the Sierra Club. He fought hard for the creation of Yosemite, but sadly lost the fight over the Hetch Hetchy

Valley. He died soon after the approval of the dam, some say from a broken heart.

Aldo Leopold

A former United States Forest Service employee and professor at the University of Wisconsin, Leopold is considered the father of wildlife management in the United States, and he contributed a great deal to the idea of wilderness preservation in America. His book, a "*Sand County Almanac*," became one of the bibles of the environmental movement of the late sixties and seventies. His son, A. Starker Leopold, became a University of California professor and wrote a landmark report to the National Park Service that shaped the manner in which park resources were managed. He suggested that they be managed in "the illusion of what parks were before the entrance of European man." Native Americans used fire to enhance hunting and employed other resource management tools, like sustained hunting, but the report did not take this into account. Starker Leopold's philosophy is used today in many agencies in this country.

Rachel Carson

Rachel Carson was a writer, an ecologist, and a scientist. She was a trained marine biologist and began her career with the United States Fish and Wildlife Service. She wrote "*Silent Spring*," a book published in 1962 that turned the heads of the most learned Americans toward what we were doing to the environment by the use of pesticides. She really started the environmental movement. Her work with pesticides, particularly DDT and its effects on the environment and on birds, was significant.

Margaret Murie

Margaret Murie was a naturalist who was dubbed the "grandmother of the conservation movement" by the Sierra Club. She helped to pass the Wilderness Act of 1964 and was instrumental in creating the Alaska National Wildlife Refuge by recruiting U.S. Supreme Court Justice William O. Douglas to help talk President Eisenhower into setting aside 140,000 acres for the refuge. She also worked to get the Alaska National Interest Lands Conservation Act which was signed by President Carter in 1980. In 1998, President Clinton awarded her the Presidential Medal of Freedom.

Teddy Roosevelt

The "Conservation President" was a huge supporter of park, forest, and wildlife preservation. Like a lot of people in that era, he was a devoted hunter, but still did much for the national parks. The United States Forest Service and the United States Fish and Wildlife Service were created during his tenure. Roosevelt was a trained ornithologist, but he became more than just a bird watcher. He created many national bird and wildlife sanctuaries and was behind the creation of the Antiquities Act of 1906, which allowed the President to set aside areas that had scientific value. It is an act that is still used today by almost every president as a part of his legacy. He created the United States Fish and Wildlife Service and saved the Grand Canyon from exploitation by making it a national monument. We must also add that Roosevelt also agreed to the damming of the Hetch Hetchy Valley in Yosemite, which caused huge damage to a once-pristine place.

Steven Mather

In his lifetime, Steven Mather did much more for the parks than just his contributions to the founding of the National Park Service and his influence in creating state parks. At the entrances of national parks everywhere are bronze plaques honoring Mather that read, "There is no end to the good he has done." To old-time rangers, his name was, and still is, spoken in awe and in reverence. In Yosemite, Mather lobbied to have a federal law changed that disallowed the donation of items to the government. After the law was successfully changed, he bought the Tioga Toll Road and gave it to the Park. Seeing where the rangers had to live in the Yosemite Valley caused him to reach into his pocket for funds to build the Ranger Club. The building is still used to house rangers today. He sold the giant railroad companies on the park idea so that they would bring rails close to parks (and in some cases into parks). It was an effort to sell the national park idea to America. Mather's favorite thing to do was to take elected government officials who were cool toward the national park idea on camping trips into the parks personally. In the summer of 1915, he took a select group of congressmen on a tour of the western parks so that they could see for themselves the natural wonders available in the parks.

When I attended Albright Training Center on sabbatical leave from teaching, one of the things that I was assigned to do before coming to the Center was to read a biography of Mather's life and Horace Albright's *Oh Ranger*. The book on Mather, *Steven Mather of the National Parks*, was written by Robert Shankland in 1951. The National Park Service needs to start requiring this type of reading again when new people are hired. The list of heroes above is a pretty good place to start, but there are many others you might include, other people who had a hand in the development of preserving and conserving the outdoors, like Horace Albright, the Park Service's second director or Gifford Pinchot, the first Forest Service director. However revered by early Forest Service employees, Pinchot did not care for recreational use of the National Forests and viewed the creation of the National Park Service as a disaster to the conservation movement because he considered it a waste of natural resources.

Modern Heroes

William Penn Mott

There are heroes at every local level in this country, but around the San Francisco Bay Area, the East Bay, and California State Parks, there is none greater than Bill Mott. Born in New York, a graduate of Michigan State University, he became a landscape architect in the National Park Service's San Francisco regional office in 1933. He intended to go into private practice, but became the Director of Parks for the City of Oakland instead, where he remained for 17 years. During this time, he hired the first naturalist in a municipal system in the country. In 1962 he left Oakland to become the Director of the East Bay Regional Park District (EBRPD). When Ronald Reagan was elected governor of California in 1967, Bill went to Sacramento to be Reagan's State Park Director. During his tenure there, the State Parks added over a thousand acres to the already very large system. He was offered the National Park Service Director position by then-President Richard Nixon, but declined.

Bill left the State Park job after Reagan's second term in office. He was 65 years old. Bill then became the Director of Parks and Recreation for the town of Moraga. He also became the CEO of the California State Parks Foundation, which he had founded in 1969. Bill accepted President Ronald Reagan's offer to become the Director of the National Park Service in 1985 and was in that position until 1989. During Bill's time as NPS Director, the Yellowstone fires happened and Bill had to defend the "let-burn" policy that was in place at the time. Bill died in 1992. He once said, "A vision is a powerful thing. It is a dream based upon a clear perception of the future combined with a commitment to take the necessary steps to make it happen."

I am pleased to say that I had an opportunity to know Bill, as well as his son John, a California State Park Ranger.

Freeman Tilden

Freeman Tilden was born in 1883 and started his writing career as a reporter for several newspapers in the eastern U.S. With the urging of National Park Director Newton Drury, he began to write about the national parks. He concentrated his writings on the purposes and objectives of national and state parks and the principles of how they were selected, managed, and used. He wrote a landmark book, *Interpreting Our Heritage*, that gave form and substance to the profession of heritage and all interpretation ever since. It was a book that I used as a text at West Valley College. Tilden gave fundamental principles that would guide park naturalists and interpreters to this day. To many people he is the "father of park interpretation" and a hero to park professionals. Freeman died in 1980 at the age of 96.

George Melendez Wright

George Wright was born in 1904 in the San Francisco Bay Area and studied famous naturalists while in college at U.C. Berkeley. That interest led George to a position as a naturalist in Yosemite National Park in 1927. At the time, resource management was not a subject that the national parks were taking very seriously. Bears were being artificially fed at garbage dumps to the delight of park visitors sitting in bleachers nearby, and predators were being disposed of in favor of hooved animals like elk. In 1930, Wright, along with two others, started a four-year survey of wildlife and plants in the national parks, which he funded out of his own pocket. This survey resulted in two landmark reports that ultimately caused the park service to abandon feeding at the dumps and killing predators. In 1933, at the age of 29, George Wright became the chief of the newly-created Wildlife Division of the National Park Service. While Wright was returning from a biological survey at Big Bend, Texas, he was tragically killed in an auto accident. He was 31 years of age. Wright was truly the "father of park resource management."

The George Wright Society was created in 1980 as a nonprofit association of researchers, administrators, educators, and park professionals who work in protected areas around the world. It was fostered to provide communication and a shared sense of purpose in order to be able to face the complex problems facing the management of resources in this modern world.[44]

Who will be Nature's New Champions?

The philosophy of setting land aside for the enjoyment of the citizens of this country has been embraced by a vast majority of the voting

---

[44] http://www.georgewright.org/

public. The battles have already been fought mostly by people like Muir, Mather, and Roosevelt.

Where are the heroes willing to face the complex problems facing parks in this modern age and in the future? Writer and historian Alfred Runte might be one of those. He was one of the major forces behind the saving of the railroad at the Grand Canyon and continues to write about the issues of the parks. Ken Burns produced a 12-hour television series about the national parks, and former directors of the National Park Service who had to stand up to presidents and a congress that could have cared less about parks. Runte was one of Ken Burn's advisors on this project. The late Huell Howser was a huge advocate for the California State Park System through his television series "California's Gold," seen on public television. People that have a profound interest in the future of parks in America have banded together to act as watchdogs, to offer advice, and to serve as avenues of communication and training. The question is, "Are the politicians listening?"

Professional Ranger Organizations

Rangers have come together because there were few carrying the torch of park management to government agencies and to the public. Associations like the National Recreation and Park Association (NRPA) and state organizations like the California Park and Recreation Society (CPRS) were tilted toward organized recreation and urban park management. I personally have attended conferences of those organizations that had little on the agenda for open space or regional parks or anything for ground level people like park rangers. In the San Francisco Bay Area, this lack was so apparent to park managers that they started the Bay Area Landscape Supervisors Forum, which met for lunch once a month to discuss the problems they were facing in urban parks. The organization included the park directors of most of the cities in the Bay Area. I often attended this group as a guest of the City of Saratoga park director, whose office was across the street from the college where I taught.

It became very apparent that there was no representation out there when 60 park rangers got to talk to each other at the coffee breaks at an in-service training session held at West Valley College in 1970. Those discussions led to the formation of the Park Ranger's Association of California (PRAC), an organization of uniformed park employees in California with a purpose of "Professionalism through unity." The California State Park Rangers Association (CSPRA) had already been formed in 1964 and was a big help in the formation of PRAC. We had a couple of state park people at our initial meetings on the lawn of a Santa Clara County park ranger, Raleigh Young, as Raleigh's wife Suzanna fed us all pizza.

The first idea about the formation of a ranger association came from Raleigh and Park Ranger Bill Lawrence of San Mateo County, who believed that the time had come for rangers to band together. Their vision was a San Francisco Bay Area organization rather than a statewide one, but that changed during the early discussions. Soon bylaws were drawn up, other organizational meetings were held, and PRAC was born. Jerry Lawrence of Palo Alto was the interim president, I was vice president and in charge of the first conference, and Walter Cacace of Santa Cruz was the secretary.

During a weekend at the end of September 1977, a group of national park rangers met in Jackson Hole, Wyoming. The purpose, at first, was social. However, talk turned to the National Park Service and all the problems the service was facing at the time. They discussed the law enforcement task force report, pondered how to evaluate seasonal rangers, shared other concerns, and explored solutions. After discussion, the group decided to form the Association of National Park Rangers (ANPR), whose purpose was to "Communicate for, and about, and with rangers; to identify, promote, and enhance our profession and its spirit, to support management and the perpetuation of the National Park Service and to provide a forum for social enrichment."

At the time of the formation of ANPR, I was president of PRAC and a seasonal ranger in Yosemite. Roger Rudolph, the secretary of the new organization, was a former supervisor of mine and was now stationed in Yellowstone. He knew of my involvement with PRAC, so Roger contacted me. I sent them a copy of the bylaws of PRAC and also told him how we conducted our conferences. As I recall, I even sent him $25 for stamps. From CSPRA to PRAC to ANPR, the professional ranger family was coming together. It has been a movement that also has created an International Federation of Park Rangers that gathers rangers from all over the world once a year for a conference. This meeting is a chance to share knowledge and to find out that most of our problems are the same.

ANPR seemed to have the most political influence, being an organization for only one agency. They have been able to have people give reports to Congress. For a time, CSPRA was the bargaining unit for California State Parks until a new organization was formed. The California State Park Peace Officers Association now represents the state park rangers. CSPRA still exists, but is a mere shadow of what it once was. The New England Park Rangers Association, the Tennessee Rangers Association, and Washington State Rangers Association are similar organizations.

There are also organizations that support those rangers that are involved strictly with law enforcement issues or where enforcement is a very large part of their jobs. Both the Park Law Enforcement Association (PLEA) and the United States Park Ranger Lodge of the Fraternal Order of Police are national organizations. Neither really have parks as a major concern. It appears the major thrust is on ranger safety.

All of the above organizations need to become more politically active in their realm of influence. A great place to start would be the annual Earth Day celebrations. Earth Day began when major environmental groups conducted study groups about the state of the world's environment. A wakeup call was needed. Earth Day every April is a great time to let the people know what rangers do, what open space is all about, and how important it is to our daily lives. There is a national audience on Earth Day. Most agencies conduct trash pickups to celebrate. Although trash pickups are needed, we need to do a lot more than that.

Another exciting organization was formed to "study, educate, speak, and act for the preservation and protection of America's national parks." In May 2003, the assistant director of the National Park Service, Destry Jarvis, was contacted by the Rockefeller Family Fund (RFF) to prepare an analysis on the "assaults on federal lands, particularly the national parks."

Mr. Jarvis placed a call to retired NPS employee Bill Wade, who in turn called on retired NPS friends Rick Smith and Mike Finely to help him with this task. The three were former NPS Supervisors, and Jarvis knew that they were well versed on the problems facing parks. Jarvis also knew that the fear of retribution would be there if he used active NPS employees. The three made their presentations at the National Press Club in Washington, D.C., on May 19th of the same year.[45]

The RFF also wanted a letter voicing similar concerns sent to President Bush and Interior Secretary Gale Norton. This letter was signed by 28 former NPS managers.[46] Of course, the original three spent many hours on the telephone following the press conference lining up the people to sign the letter. After the letter was released, there was a groundswell of interest among other retirees. Because of that large show of interest, the letter was re-released with more than 60 signers. After this experience, it was realized that a group of retirees was needed, and from that first group of letter signers, a new organization was born and incorporated in 2006.[47]

Since that time, the Coalition to Protect America's National Parks (CNANP) has grown to over 1000 members who support the mission of the National Park Service. If you believe in the edict that as the NPS goes, so goes everyone else, then I really think that this new organization has the political power to get things done on a national level. First and foremost, the members are retired and untouchable. They can voice their opinions without fear of reprisal. Most importantly, the members are experts. They have already testified on behalf of the organization in front of Congress and supported several issues facing

---

[45] Email correspondence with Bill Wade, July 6, 2013.
[46] Coalition to Protect America's National Parks http://www.protectnps.org
[47] Op. cit.

management of national parks like the use of snowmobiles in Yellowstone.

In 2005, CPANP members began to hear a rumor that a person in the Interior Department was proposing to rewrite some 2001 NPS management policies. Assured that the changes were to be very minor by higher ups, members of CPANP obtained a copy and found out that was not the case. Not even close. There had been a long standing tradition that such rewrites were to just update policies rather to change the mission. This rewrite was certainly going to make major changes. A major campaign was undertaken by CPANP to stop this attempt. Emails were sent out to park superintendents, the media was contacted, and a cooperative partnership was obtained with the National Park and Conservation Association. The effort by Interior ceased.

Citizen's Groups

Of course, there are many citizen groups nationwide that lobby for parks and open space. The Sierra Club, the Wilderness Society, the National Parks and Conservation Association and the Audubon Society are four such groups on a national level. All four spend large amounts of dollars lobbying Congress, state legislatures, local boards, and city council members. The Nature Conservancy purchases open space lands all over the world. Also national, state, and local foundations not only support parks with dollars, but also provide huge political support.

I am also sure that around the country there are organizations similar to the Committee of Green Foothills that is active in our county. This committee has been powerful in the ability to keep development from the boundaries of our parks and open spaces.

World Park Congress

The World Park Congress is organized every ten years by the International Union for the Conservation of Nature to share knowledge and to set the agenda for the next ten years to conserve natural protected areas. It met this past fall and it included members of the International Ranger Federation that consists of the ranger organizations that are mentioned above (PRAC CSPRA, ANPR) plus ranger organizations from all over the world. In November of 2014, the Congress met in Sydney, Australia, and included delegates from 170 nations. Protecting park rangers, so essential to protecting parks, was high on the agenda list.

The saviors may be many.

Park rangers have had an interesting evolution. As society and issues facing the parks have changed, park rangers and their future have also undergone change. In the next section, we'll look at the history of park rangers and the challenges they will face in future years.

Section 2

Growth of the Park Ranger Profession in America and the Role of the Ranger

A Yosemite training session with the California
Highway Patrol in the 1970's
(Photo by Tom Habecker)

Chapter 7: The Park Ranger: Protectors of Our Natural, Cultural and Historical Heritage

We have tried to present why we have open space and the reasons why agencies were formed in all their different jurisdictions to protect those lands from exploitation. As the parks were created, rangers appeared, and they quickly became a part of the culture of the outdoors. The public wanted to use the lands for recreation, which created the need for protection of land from use and of the users from each other. Rangers filled the need.

When the Park Rangers Association of California (PRAC) was first formed, the founding fathers had a discussion about who was qualified to be in the new organization, and tried to define just what a ranger was. The descriptions of rangers varied from organization to organization within the State of California. Finally the Association decided it would be "any uniformed park employee." In some agencies, rangers were maintenance people, some were naturalists, some were law enforcement personnel, and some were all three, or a variety of the three. To the public, if you worked in a park, you were "rangers."

The First Rangers

With tongue in cheek, one of my former students who is now a ranger in the National Park Service sent me an article written in the *Thin Green Line*, the journal of the International Park Ranger Federation. It included a paragraph that appeared in *Parks and Recreation* magazine in November, 1994. It said, "Contrary to popular belief, the oldest profession is that of being a park ranger. At least that is what one Oklahoma judge claimed. He equated the job with the cherubic guard placed at the Biblical Garden of Eden to protect it from the only two people in the world!"

It is believed by some that the word "ranger" seems to correspond to the Medieval Latin word "regardatores," which appeared in 1217 in the Charter of the Forest.[48] The term "ranger" has been used over the centuries by many organizations to describe a person or persons whose duty it was to protect either people or the environment.

The first use of the title "Ranger" was believed to have been in the English Rolls of Parliament in 1455. The "English Royal Ranger" was the officer appointed by the King "to patrol the royal forests and parks, preventing trespass and poaching, and assisted in the royal hunt."[49]

Sir Walter Scott wrote in Rokely: "He heard the rangers' loud halloo, beating each cover while they came, As if to start the sylvan game."

Spencer wrote in 1579 about the ranger and the royal hunt in Sheph; he wrote, "Wolves walk not widely, as they were woont. For fear of rangers, and the great hoont."[50]

The use of the word "ranger" came to be used by other organizations, such as the military, the Texas Highway Patrol, and the rangers in the national forests and in parks agencies all over this country and all over the world. It is in the form of the English meaning that we can follow the evolution of the park ranger in America.

The Ranger and the American Colonial Period

In the early years of this country, the ranger's job was to protect the people from the hazards of living on the frontier and especially from the Indians. The "ranger" position was a transplant from England during colonization. *The Pennsylvania Gazette* in 1744 called upon "Any person or persons, who have lost one or more of the following strays, (lost animals) by applying to William Hartley, of Charles Town, Chief Ranger for Chester County ... proving their lawful property ... may be informed where to find them."[51] Mr. Hartley could be

---

[48] Charles R. Young, *The Royal Forest of Medieval England,* University of Pennsylvania Press, 1979, p. 163.
[49] John W. Hennenberger, Albright Training Center Handout, *The Evolution of the National Park Ranger,* date unknown.
[50] Hennenberger, op. cit.
[51] Hennenberger, op. cit., p. 4.

the first ranger in America, and his title implies that there might have been others. Later the term "ranger" was enlarged to mean a body of armed mounted men who were employed to range over an area to protect the colony from the Indians.[52]

The earliest records report rangers as paid soldiers for the protection of the frontier in 1742, when the Provisions for the Colony of Georgia recorded that "for the defense of the colony...it is necessary to have rangers who can ride the wood."[53]

Before the Revolutionary War, rangers were organized into militia units. These units were placed into the Continental Army and fought for our independence from Europe. General George Washington ordered Lieutenant Colonel Thomas Knowlton to select an elite group of men for reconnaissance missions. "Knowlton's Rangers," were the first military unit to use the title of ranger. Since then, every war in which this country has participated, from the Revolution to the Iraq War, has had ranger battalions serving bravely in our armed forces.

The State of Virginia in 1796 sent out men they called rangers into the forests against the Cherokee Indians. The American frontier soldier, Robert Rogers, raised and commanded a force of militia that became known as the "Rogers Rangers." This group was known for its courage during the French and Indian Wars.

The Ranger Heads West

The ranger expanded west with the rest of the country. Almost every state had a ranger organization to protect themselves from the Native Americans. Rangers also served as a police force in many states. There were ranger companies that were authorized by Congress for protection. They were different than the Rogers Rangers, however. *Harper's* magazine, in 1857, described this system as one where each person acts in concert with his fellows, yet fights on his own.[54] The Texas

---

[52] Hennenberger, op. cit., p. 4.
[53] Hennenberger, op. cit., p. 4.
[54] Hennenburger op. cit., p. 5.

Rangers used this type of system in protecting the citizens there. The Texas Rangers had no specific uniform and no official law enforcement policies or procedures. The period when the Texas Rangers were patrolling their state became an important period in the evolution of the ranger as a modern law enforcement officer.

Park Ranger Name Comes From California

Many of the new forest reserves that were created by the Federal Government lay next to national parks. Protection of the forest reserves was handled by the Federal General Land Office and the overall administration of both parks and forests was handled by the Department of the Interior.

Some historians say that Yosemite became the first California State Park when the Federal Government turned the park over to the state to operate in 1864. Other people say that Big Basin State Park was the first California State Park because Yosemite was only "loaned" to the state by the Federal Government. Big Basin Redwood State Park was created in 1905. Some people even call Yosemite the first National Park over Yellowstone because the Yosemite land was set aside in 1864, eight years before Yellowstone. If one believes in that concept, then Galen Clark would have been the first national park ranger, and not Harry Yount. Galen Clark became a "Guardian of Yosemite" in 1866 and the first California State Park Ranger, and good old Harry not until 1880. This argument will certainly continue.

Because there had been destruction of trees, defacing of "natural objects," and the wanton setting of fires, the first park laws appeared in Yosemite in 1866. These laws led to the creation of the protective position of "Guardian."[55] Galen Clark was named the first "Guardian of Yosemite" in May of 1866 and served in this position for 22 years.

---

[55] Michael G. Lynch, *Rangers of California State Parks*, Arcadia Publishing, 1996.

Galen Clark

Born in Canada in 1814, Clark went to Wawona (now in Yosemite) for health reasons. He had been diagnosed with tuberculosis at age 39 and thought that being in the mountains might cure him. Instead, he discovered the Mariposa Grove of Big Trees and spent time teaching others about that mighty grove of Sequoias and the land that would be Yosemite National Park. After writing several letters to Congress about preserving the area, he finally got the support of California Senator John Conness, who pushed a bill through Congress. When the Yosemite Grant was signed into law by President Abraham Lincoln, Clark became the Grant's guardian.

Harry Yount

Little is known about Yount's early life, but thanks to some National Park Service historians, he is remembered as being the first ranger in a National Park when he was hired to protect Yellowstone. Harry Yount was believed to have been born in Missouri, perhaps in 1837. Harry enlisted in the Union Army during the Civil War, was wounded, captured, and held for 28 days before being exchanged.[56] After the Civil War, Harry came to Wyoming Territory and served on the Bozeman Trail as a "bull whacker." He also worked as a hunter, trapper, guide, and scout.[57] As a buffalo hunter, he earned a dollar per animal. The second superintendent of Yellowstone, Philetus Norris, hired Yount as a gamekeeper because such a slaughter of animals was taking place that they needed protection. Yount received $1000 a year. The money came from the meager budget given to the park by Congress. Because of Yount's ability to survive in Yellowstone's winter climate, he became the first white man known to have spent the winter there. Because Yount suggested that a "ranger force" be hired to

---

[56] William R. Supernaugh, "Enigmatic Icon; The Life and Times of Harry Yount," *Annals of Wyoming, The Wyoming History Journal*, Spring 1998, 70 No 2, Wyoming State Historical Society 1998.
[57] Supernaugh, op. cit.

protect the park, he might be credited with being the father of the park ranger service. Even though his tenure in Yellowstone was short (14 months), Yount left such a lasting legacy that the National Park Service honors one person every year with the Harry Yount Award for being the ranger who best represents what national park rangers should be: the ranger's ranger. I have been very lucky to have known three such recipients. Yount died in 1924 as a result of "suspended heart action."

The United States Cavalry Comes to the Rescue

When the Congress of the United States created Yellowstone National Park in 1872, they did not provide any methods of protection, nor did they even give the new park funds to hire anyone. One person, first Superintendent Nathaniel P. Langford, watched over Yellowstone Park. The tourists who visited Yellowstone poached wildlife and did considerable damage to the geological features. Langford appointed David Folsom to look after the park in 1873. Three years later, Langford designated James McCartney as a custodian for the summer. Could Mr. McCartney have been the first seasonal ranger? Harry Yount was hired as a gamekeeper in 1880 and has been considered to be the first full time national park ranger.[58] The job to protect Yellowstone was so overwhelming that Yount soon gave up. He did suggest that the government appoint a small police force to enforce the rules and regulations of the park. The operations were so ineffective that Congress refused to spend any more money on Yellowstone. Since the United States was not at war and the Cavalry was available, the Secretary of the Interior called upon the military to help out. In August 1886, the Cavalry entered Yellowstone with the job of protecting the park. Fort Yellowstone was established and outposts were provided.

---

[58] Charles R. Farabee, *National Park Ranger, an American Icon*, Roberts Reinhart, 2003.

The author giving a living history presentation on the
Cavalry as they were in 1896 in Yosemite National Park.
(Photo by Thomas Habecker)

The same problems that existed in Yellowstone National Park were also present in Yosemite. Vast herds of sheep and cattle grazed the meadows of the park, and miners prospected the mountains and valleys. Poachers were also killing off the wildlife in alarming numbers. Since the precedent had been set in Yellowstone, the Cavalry was asked to come to the rescue. They came to Yosemite each spring from San Francisco Presidio. The troops actually gave nature walks, established a nature museum in Yosemite Valley, cut and burned slash to prevent large forest fires, built trails, mapped the Park, and created entrance stations to take firearms away from visitors. The Cavalry gave us our "ranger Stetson" hat, which is a symbol of the ranger profession.[59] The Cavalry also created their own poaching problem when the troops began shooting deer to supplement their army diet, so their commanding officers took away their weapons.

---

[59] Thomas A. Smith, *I'm Just a Seasonal,* Productivity Productions, Rochester, New York, 2005.

The army had a huge place in the evolution of the ranger profession and the activities they provided have become part of the park culture in this country. Even to this day, some park agency rangers around the United States use military descriptions for their positions. Captain's bars and chevrons are starting to appear on collars and the sleeves of uniforms. Many of the Cavalry joined the park ranger ranks when the National Park Service was created.

The Rise of Rules and Enforcement

If you believe that wearing a badge, enforcement of the law, or the carrying of weapons is something new for a park ranger, you would be in error.

Rangers have always been the park protectors. In fact, one of the very first, if not the first, law enforcement agency in the United States was the United States Park Police, established in 1791 to watch over the National Capital grounds and the surrounding area in Washington, D.C. In a sense, these "watchmen" were the very first park protectors. We have already alluded to the fact that when Yellowstone National Park appeared in 1872 and visitors started to come to see its wondrous features, some bad things started to happen. Damage and vandalism started to appear at some of the geyser basins, and rampant poaching of wildlife occurred. It was obvious that some kind of enforcement actions had to take place.

The Yellowstone Act gave the Secretary of the Interior the power to publish rules and regulations and "Such regulations shall provide for the preservation, from injury or spoliation, of all timber, mineral deposits, natural curiosities, or wonders within said park, and their retention in their natural condition." In addition, the Secretary was to "provide against wanton destruction of the fish and game found within said park and against their capture or destruction for the purposes of merchandise or profit."[60] The Act went on to say that "the

---

[60] Albright Training Center handout, Author and date unknown.

Secretary shall cause all persons trespassing… to be removed there from."

Carl Schurz was the Secretary of Interior and he published rules in 1877 prohibiting hunting and fishing except to provide recreation or food for the park visitors.

Nathaniel Langford, the first Superintendent of Yellowstone, was faced with huge problems. Langford created a set of rules designed to curb the hunting, fishing, trapping, and the cutting of timber or the collection of specimens without permission of the Superintendent. He also told the people who were living within the boundaries that they had to vacate the park. Langford became very frustrated because he was alone and really had no power to do very much, so the destruction continued.

Harry Yount was eventually hired to take over the enforcement and to try to stop the vandalism and the destruction that was taking place. He had 10 assistants in 1881 to help him stop the cutting of timber, the removal of mineral deposits, the hunting, fishing, trapping, and the sale of intoxicating liquors. They also had to remove trespassers. They were at a loss about how and where to start to do all they were supposed to do. During this period of time, the Army was active in the area fighting the war against the Plains Indians and was available. There were some members of Congress who did not think that was appropriate use of military troops. However in 1886, Troop M of the U.S. Cavalry arrived to set up camp. The era of the cavalry lasted for 32 years!

The Forest Ranger

The passage of the Federal Forest Reserve Act of 1891 set aside large timberland reserves from the public domain. The reserves were generally closed to public use. The main reasons that they were taken out of the public domain was to protect the watersheds, to preserve a source of supply of timber for the nation, and to keep them from private exploitation.

In the beginning, personnel assigned to the forest reserves were land agents of the General Land Office. Congress passed an act in 1897 that outlined a system of organization and management of the reserves. The forest ranger title appeared at that time to describe the "man on the ground." "On the ground" is a term still used in the Forest Service to describe the front-line people working in the outdoors, doing their job. In 1898, these rangers were placed in special districts and were assigned to patrol the reserves, prevent forest fires, and to assist in the management of the forests.[61]

The three California National Parks, Yosemite, General Grant, and Sequoia, were right next to the Sequoia Forest Reserve, which was established in 1875. The Army, which had been called upon to protect the parks, had to abandon their protection in 1898 because of the Spanish/American war, and the Federal General Land Office had to then assume the protection duties. A "special land inspector" was assigned to keep the poachers, miners, and sheep herders out of the parks. In the fall of 1898, the Cavalry returned to their park protection duties but only served during the summer months. When the Cavalry returned to the Presidio of San Francisco for the winter, that left the parks unprotected. The General Land Office recommended that "forest rangers" be hired like those in the adjacent forest reserve to take care of and protect the parks until the Army returned in the spring.

Archie C. Leonard and Charles A. Leidig were hired as forest rangers in the fall of 1898 to work in Yosemite, and Ernest Britten was put to work in Sequoia National Park in 1890. Britten had actually protected Sequoia National Park from 1888 to 1890 as part of his regular job in the forest reserve. When the Army returned, these men reported to the commanding officers and continued to work under their supervision. In 1901 Army reports from Sequoia to the Secretary of the Interior started referring to these men as "park rangers" and not forest rangers. Their title was officially changed to park ranger shortly after

---

[61] *Report of the Commissioner of the GLO Annual report of the Department of Interior.* 1899. Patrol of Reserves, 101-103.

the summer of 1905.[62] It was the first time that the term "park ranger" officially had been used. Two years later the rangers took over from the Army and were patrolling all the natural parks, national monuments, and historic sites as well.

In 1894, Yellowstone had a jail and a magistrate. In 1905, its first arrest authority. In 1915, "Regulations Governing Rangers in the National Parks," was issued by General Superintendent Mark Daniels. A separate ranger service was provided when the Park Service was created in the Organic Act of 1916. The Organic Act of 1916 not only created the National Park Service, but gave direction to the new administration as to how they were to manage the new system. They were to be managed to "conserve the resources, wildlife, and historic objects therein and provide use of the same by such manner and such means as will leave them unimpaired for the enjoyment of future generations." This statement would later become a real issue with managers because of the statement requiring use that still keeps them unimpaired. The provision is still an issue today.

The Profession Evolves

As the park ranger profession evolved in the national parks like Yosemite, Yellowstone, and Sequoia, other agencies in the country picked up the concept. Counties and municipalities began park agencies. Regional parks appeared in the 1920's, like the East Bay Regional Park District which encompasses two counties in the San Francisco Bay Area, and the Santa Clara County Department of Parks and Recreation. Each had its "first ranger." San Jose, California's first park, Alum Rock, was created in the late 1860s, but it took a very long time before they hired a ranger. Their first ranger, Max McKlintock, was hired in the 1970s to "clean up" Alum Rock Park. Alum Rock, a large regional park, was once a nice place to bring your family, but had been taken over by a lawless element that had been having dogfights and drug dealings. The presence of Ranger McKlintock just caused

---

[62] John Hennenberger, "The Evolution of the Park Ranger" An Albright Training Center Handout, date unknown.

the troublemakers to move to a nearby county park. The problem then shifted to the rangers there.

Seasonal Rangers: The "Ninety Day Wonders"

In the early years of the National Parks, visitation was most often only during the summer months. School was out, and families had the time to travel, camp, and explore the outdoors. Fulltime rangers could easily be overwhelmed by too many park visitors and too few rangers. Harry Yount had even suggested in 1881 that a force of men should be hired on a temporary basis to help manage Yellowstone.[63] Not long after that, the National Park Service began to hire people for just the high tourist season. These people would usually only work the three or four months that school was out, from Memorial Day to Labor Day. Most were students and teachers. One was even to become the President of the United States. Gerald R. Ford spent a summer in Yellowstone as a seasonal ranger in 1936.

In the early days, if the superintendent liked what he saw in a seasonal, he could hire them on the spot. Many old-timers began their careers in this manner. I doubt very much whether any park visitor could tell the difference between a seasonal and permanent, fulltime staff. Most open permanent positions are still being filled by seasonal rangers. Most seasonal rangers are now students bent on a fulltime position who may spend several years in a seasonal position in several parks before that happens. For some, a fulltime position may never happen.

Many of the first permanent employees did not like to work with seasonal rangers. In the early days, some seasonal rangers were political appointees who thought it was "nice" to work in a national park in the summer, and they came with no skills to survive in an outdoor environment. Permanent employees just didn't want to have to train people year after year, so they hated the political appointees. They sarcastically called them "ninety day wonders." or "college boys." I

---

[63] Farabee, op. cit., p.143.

often thought that another reason that permanent rangers didn't like "ninety day wonders" was that the seasonal ranger was doing the jobs that the full-timer loved to do. The permanents were stuck in the office doing paperwork. The seasonal cadre that I worked with in the '70s and '80s in the Mather District of Yosemite was very stable. They were an "old guard," returning to work summer after summer. Most seasonal rangers in those days provided more continuity year after year since they were more long term than permanent rangers. Permanent rangers were usually here today, gone to another park tomorrow. For the most part, most full time rangers transfer to other parks in order to move up in the system. Although it is somewhat rare, some just stay in the same park for their careers. Seasonal rangers actually had to train some new permanents every year, not the other way around.

Yosemite historian Jim Snyder has said that Clyde Quick, an old-time Yosemite seasonal, had told him that he always had to train a new district and assistant district ranger, that they would be in charge, but he and the other seasonal rangers would have to show them what to do and how to get around the country. He would get them "trained" and then they would transfer, so Clyde and the others would have to start all over again the next summer.[64]

Almost every year I worked in Yosemite, I had an immediate supervisor who was either new to the park or new to Tuolumne Meadows. Most did not know where the best places were to land a helicopter, where people walked out when they were lost in places like Porcupine Flat, what our biggest enforcement problem was, and what was the quickest way to get from one place to another.

With the cultural change in recent years, it is a rare event to graduate from a college into a fulltime position with any park agency without having seasonal experience first. In some park agencies, in order to get seasonal employment you must have law enforcement training given at either a police academy or one of the NPS seasonal academies. Few academies talk about park culture, so new seasonal rangers

---

[64] Jim Snyder, written correspondence to author dated October 23, 1996.

now are entering the profession with a law enforcement focus from the very beginning.

In a real sense, not much has been written about the evolution of the ranger to what we have today. One such document that comes quickly to mind is a book entitled *Protecting Paradise*, written by Shirley Sargent, who wrote about the rangers that worked in Yosemite from 1898 until 1960. Charles "Butch" Farabee's *National Park Ranger, an American Icon*, is an excellent historical resource about how national park rangers evolved.

There are several personal memoirs written by national park rangers in the early days:

- *Recollections of a Rocky Mountain Ranger*, by Jack Moomaw is one such document. Jack first started his career as a seasonal ranger in 1921, got a full time job with the National Parks in 1922, and retired in 1945.

- *Guardians of Yosemite*, by John Bingaman is another fine book on the early rangers in Yosemite. It covers the same time period as Moomaw.

- My own book, *I'm Just a Seasonal*, published in 2005, covers a time period in the '70s and '80s when most seasonal rangers were teachers and students.

- Former Chief Ranger in Yellowstone, Dan Sholly, wrote *Guardians of Yellowstone*, which is a more modern book about the life and times of a ranger in that great park, including an excellent exposé of the politics of the Yellowstone fires.

- *A Park Rangers Life*, by 32-year national park veteran Bruce Bytmar, covers the years up to the attacks on 9/11.

- From a state park point of view, Mike Lynch's book on *Rangers of California's State Parks* is a great resource about how a state park agency and its rangers evolved.

A resource list of books for more serious study is available in Appendix A.

Chapter 8: The Ranger Job Description

As parks were developed by a variety of government entities and populations grew, the job of the ranger has remained basically the same over the years. Of course that depends upon where the ranger is working and for which agency.

Certainly improvements in technology, like better vehicles, radios, and computers, have made the job easier. When I began my seasonal career in 1970 as a backcountry ranger in Yosemite, I had a five-watt radio that weighed 9 pounds, needed 18 batteries, and had to be carried in a saddlebag. When I left the Service after 15 summers, technology had given us radios with the same range of service that were three inches wide by about eight inches long, weighed very little, and were powered by one small battery. I could carry it on my belt. The old helicopters had trouble flying in the light air at high altitude. The new ones could now land and lift off of the top of Mount Whitney, from over 14,000 feet. Not long after my career ended, computers were on every desk.

The other thing that changed is the emphasis placed on each aspect of the job, and whether a ranger is a specialist or a generalist.

A 1926 National Park Service Seasonal Job Description

The following cover letter was written before the season of 1926 by Superintendent of the Park, Horace Albright, and went along with an application for employment as a seasonal ranger in Yellowstone National Park. Mr. Albright would become the second Director of the National Park Service in 1929, taking over from Steven Mather. The letter is transcribed from a copy that appeared in the fall 2005 issue of *The Ranger Journal*, a publication of the Association of National Park Rangers. It appeared in the *Journal* because of the huge discussion over whether the national park ranger should continue to foster the generalist image that it had carried over the years. This description is an example of how a generalist was defined in that era. It is interesting to note that an applicant had to submit a picture of himself in "outdoor costume." That is something that an employer could not request today.

Department of Interior, National Park Service
Yellowstone National Park, Yellowstone Park, Wyoming

Office of the Superintendent

Dear Mr. _____

We have received your letter indicating your desire to become a ranger in Yellowstone National Park for the season of 1926. Before giving it further consideration, we ask you to read this circular letter very carefully and thoughtfully, and if you are still interested in the ranger position after completing your study of this communication, fill out the enclosed blank and return it to the park headquarters with a picture of yourself.

In General
It has been our experience that young men often apply for a place on the park ranger force with the impression or understanding that the ranger is a sort of sinecure with nothing resembling hard work to perform, and that the beauties and wonders of Yellowstone Park, and the frequent trips about the park and innumerable dances and other diversions to occupy one's leisure hours.

Again, young men apply for ranger positions with the feeling that the duties require no special training or experience and that any man with a reasonably good education can perform these duties regardless of whether he had a good or bad personality or whether he has or has not experience in outdoor activities. Also, many young men apply for ranger positions in the hope that making and saving considerable money to aid them in continuing their college work.

The conceptions of the duties of the ranger as just mentioned are just as untrue as it is possible for them to be, and unfortunately the pay is so small that boys earning their way through college and who live at a distance from the Park cannot afford to be a park ranger if tendered a place.

The Ranger Job
The term of service of a temporary ranger is three months from June 15th, but the superintendent has the authority to reduce the force at any time he believes it to be of interest of the Government to do this. However, a ranger can be assured of 75 days of employment.

The pay is $100.00 per month. The applicant must pay his own travel expenses to and from the Park, and must subsist himself in the Park. He must furnish his own clothes, <u>including a uniform costing about $45.00</u>. He must bring his own bed. The Government pays each man $100.00 per month and furnished quarters, light and fuel, also certain articles of furniture including a bunk, tables, dishes, cooking utensils, etc.

The ranger usually must do his own cooking and always has to care for the station. In certain places, rangers must board with road crews which are furnished very plain, but wholesome food at $1.00 per person per day.

We make no promises regarding transportation around the park to see its wonders, and often rangers do not get a chance to see all of the Park unless they are granted leave from their duties and make their own arrangements for the trip. Men who render excellent service and are retained until the close of the season are given an opportunity to tour the Park if facilities are available, otherwise not. If you apply, do not do so with the expectation that you will surely see more than the part of the Park you traverse in reaching your station.

Qualifications of a Ranger

Applicants for a ranger's position <u>must be 21 years of age</u> or must attain that age by June 15th. If you are not 21 or will not be by June 15th, don't apply. If you have the reputation of appearing unusually youthful or immature for a man of 21, don't apply. We want men who are mature in appearance. We prefer men of 25 to 30 years of age.

The ranger is primarily a policemen, therefore he should be big of frame, tall, and of average weight for his age and height. We always prefer big men to small men, other conditions being equal. If you are small in stature, better not apply.

The ranger comes more closely in contact with the visiting public than any other park officer, and he is the representative of the Secretary of Interior, the Director of the National Park Service, and the Superintendent of the Park in dealing with the public. Naturally, therefore, the ranger <u>must have a pleasing personality; he must be tactful, diplomatic and courteous; he must be patient.</u> If you are not possessed of such characteristics, please don't apply. Without them you would become, if selected, a failure from the beginning of your service.

The ranger is often called upon to guide large parties of tourists and to lecture them on the features of the Park. He should have a good strong voice and experience in public speaking. Detail public speaking and training on the application form.

The ranger is charged with the protection of the natural features of the park and especially the forests. Applicants should present evidence of their having experience in camping out in the woods. Forestry students who have had training in forestry work and forest fire training are given preference to other applicants if they possess the qualifications as to age, size and personality. The ranger must be qualified to ride and care for horses.

The ranger must know how to cook ordinary foods and must have experience in kitchen police. If you cannot cook and care for a ranger station, don't apply. You would be an unpopular burden on your fellow rangers and the butt of all station jokes should you be selected without this essential qualification.

We want big, mature men with fine personalities, and experience in the out-of-doors in riding, camping, woodcraft, fighting fires, and similar activities.

Duties of a Ranger
The ranger force is the park police force, and is on duty night and day in the protection of the Park. Protection work primarily relates to the care of forests, the fish and game, the geyser and hot spring formations and the camp grounds. Of equal importance is the detection of violations of the speed rules.

The ranger force is the information-supplying organization. The issuance of publications, answering of questions, lecturing, and guiding are all accomplished by rangers.

The ranger force is charged with the care of government property; hence much watch the use of such property by other government men as well as constantly care for the ranger stations and other property by the ranger organization itself.

Routine of the Ranger Station
Rangers must rise at 6:00 a.m. if not on night duty, and must retire not later than 11:00 p.m. They may attend dances or other entertainment not more than two evenings a week. They must obey every order of their station chief, who is a permanent ranger. Semi-military discipline is in effect at al times. A ranger is on duty from the time he arises until he retires, and may even be called from his bed for emergency service. He is not subject to an eight-hour day, and he is not paid for services rendered in excess of an eight-hour period.

In Conclusion
The ranger who renders satisfactory service is a busy man all the time. There is no vacation about his work. The duties are exacting and require utmost patience and tact at all times. A ranger's job is no place for a nervous, quick-tempered man, not for one who is unaccustomed to hard work. If you cannot work ten or twelve hours a day, and always with patience and a smile on your face, don't fill out the attached form.

Carefully reflect on what you have just read. You have perhaps believed Government jobs to be "soft" and "easy." Most of them are not, and certainly there are no such jobs in the National Park Service. The ranger's job is especially hard. There will be no more than 20 vacancies in next year's force of rangers and there is very little chance of your being considered unless you possess all of the qualifications mentioned herein. Please do not return the enclosed blank unless you believe you are fully qualified and unless you mean business. Remember there is no vacation in work, and mighty little money. If you want to come for pleasure you will be disappointed. If you want a summer in the Park as an experience in outdoor activity amid forests and fine invigorating atmosphere, apply if you are qualified, otherwise plan to visit Yellowstone National Park as a tourist.

If you apply and are accepted, no promises will be made as to the station to which you will be assigned, nor will promises be made as to assignment to foot, horse, or motorcycle patrol. You will be examined upon reporting for duty on June 15th, and will be assigned to the station having duties that we feel you can best perform.

Do not apply unless you are positive that you can report June 15th and remain until September 15th. If there is a chance of your not reporting, if accepted, we do not want your application.

If you have special qualifications which cannot be listed on the attached blank, write them on a separate sheet of paper. Send us a picture of yourself in out-door costume if possible. Otherwise a portrait will be acceptable. Picture must be clear. [65]

Cordially yours

Horace M Albright
Superintendent

In some parks today, knowing how to ride a horse and pack a mule is still necessary, but although most of today's rangers may not have to know how to ride and care for a horse and pack a mule, the other portions of this letter certainly describe, in great detail, what a generalist ranger should be, even to being paid in "sunsets." The pay wasn't much, and it still isn't, although it is better than it used to be. Taking

---

[65] Superintendent Horace Albright, Cover letter for Ranger Applicants in Yellowstone National Park, *1926, A Journal of the Association of National Park Rangers*, Vol.21 No.4., Fall 2005.

care of the ranger station and being able to survive in a backcountry situation is also important today.

The letter transcribed above leads you to believe that the present job is like that of 90 years ago. Rangers were asked to do many things at some financial sacrifice. Although seasonal rangers these days in the national parks are provided a uniform allowance, the sacrifices are still there. The allowances are seldom enough to last a season. The high altitude of Tuolumne bleached our shirts from the NPS gray to almost a dirty white over a summer. For horse patrolmen, uniform allowances are never enough. Horses are hard on clothes, and rangers are usually outdoors most of the time, exposed to the elements. By the end of the summer, the straw ranger "Stetson" would have lost its shape from getting wet and turned a very light tan from exposure from the sun. New hats had to be purchased almost every summer. We protected those hats with a passion. They are not cheap! Some rangers even bought their own tack for their horse to ensure they had the comfort every year of having good equipment and not what was left over when things were picked over in the Yosemite Valley. Most of the rangers brought their own weapons. The "service weapons" owned by the Park Service left much to be desired.

When I was first hired as a backcountry ranger and again as a front country horse patrolman, I was given a job description that spelled out in detail the knowledge, skills, and abilities that I needed and what I was going to be evaluated on at the end of the summer. It was a generalist description. The job description for a seasonal park ranger (horse patrol) in Yosemite for 1980 was almost the same as that in the Albright letter. There were few differences. We had to have a federal law enforcement commission. The early rangers did not. The size and body structure of a person obviously is not an issue now. The rest of the job description was similar. The description continued on with the knowledge that a ranger must have to be a part of this position, including knowing national park rules and regulations, law enforcement knowledge, medical and medical transport methods, knowledge of the various common written forms used, knowledge of acceptable public contact profile and demeanor, and the ability to work with little or no supervision. As a mounted ranger, I had to also know a little bit about taking care of horses.

Also included was a section on the complexity of the position. This part was about being able to respond to situations in a professional manner to people who were often unpredictable, hostile, fearful, confused, or agitated due to physical and/or emotional crisis. Although over fifty years had passed, the difference between the description written by Albright and the 1980 description was not really very great.

The Yosemite description continued to include the physical demands of the job. At the time, each ranger was required to pass a fitness test prior to the season using Cooper's Aerobic Standards or a Forest Service Step Test because the job sometimes required working long hours, sometimes in bad weather and hazardous terrain. In order to rate at an excellent level in my age group, I had to run 1.5 miles under 11 minutes or walk three miles in less than 30 minutes. I ran all winter to maintain that level of fitness.

It also should be noted that in this modern era, many fine rangers are women. The National Park Service, California State Parks, and county parks have had women as directors, including the former Director of the Santa Clara County Department of Parks and Recreation. My last year in Tuolumne, my supervisor was a woman and one of the best rangers I had worked for. She often backed me up and I was glad she did! A good book written by National Park Ranger Andrea Lankford, entitled *"Ranger Confidential,"* shows the trials and tribulations that she went through in an environment that had been traditionally male. She and other female rangers had to prove themselves many times over and sometimes were not trusted with simple tasks. The book is an "eyebrow raiser." I personally feel that women are now very much accepted in the profession.

Chapter 9: The Many Complex Roles of Park Rangers

The Enforcement Ranger

The protection of human life and park resources has been the basic mission or essence of park protection for nearly the past 100 years. While the concept and objective of protection "to shield from injury or harm" remains relevant and unchanged, parks have experienced both distinct and dramatic changes in the tools, techniques and scope and program thrusts toward meeting their protection responsibilities.[66]

The most important duty of a ranger is that of keeping people safe when they are visiting the parks. Michael Frome, in his book, *Regreening the National Parks,* says that law enforcement is now a major activity in national parks with a new breed of ranger equipped with mace, side arms, shotguns, and vehicles with light bars.[67] After a woman was stabbed to death in Yosemite Valley, rangers were warning women to not walk alone. Frome mentions how sad a situation it is when that has to happen in our parks, and he is right. However, Yosemite Valley is pretty much urban. In the summer the Valley is a like a small mobile community of several thousand people. Protection is the major function of rangers there.

Most park agencies throughout the country have rangers well trained in law enforcement. Ohio and New York have rangers whose entire job is that of enforcing the law. An article for PLEA (Park Law Enforcement Association) by a ranger from the Clark County, Ohio Park District tells about what a ranger is in Ohio. The ranger was recruited into the position from being a trained police officer and makes no mention of protecting resources. He states that "other people" know about plant life and other "scientific things." In certain parks in Cali-

---

[66] James Brady, "Developing a Resource and Visitor Protection Program (a Management Strategy for) National and State Parks and Related Protected Areas," a training document given to the Texas State Park Rangers.
[67] Michael Frome, "*Regreening the National Parks,*" University of Arizona Press, Tucson, Arizona, 1992.

fornia and elsewhere, rangers find little time for anything else but law enforcement. Parks became situational and site specific. The closer to an urban environment a park is, the higher the moral priority is to protect the people from other people, because more incidents occur.

Missouri had 43 state parks in their system and did not get around to creating park rangers until 1967. They did so because of rising enforcement issues caused by rising numbers of visitors. In the beginning, rangers had to provide their own weapons. They had to keep them locked in their vehicles during the daylight hours but could wear them at night.[68] They also had to use their own citizen's band radios to get backup help from local agencies. That situation continued until 1998, when the Highway Patrol provided radio services. Before that time, the rangers had to use local police dispatchers. By 1999, all rangers had received 470 hours of training, giving them full peace officer status.

In my training, I was always taught several basic concepts about being a park ranger beyond the usual people skills that you had to have to be successful. These skills were called the "Four P's of Protection." I had first heard this concept when Jim Brady, the former chief ranger for the entire National Park Service, gave a talk to 60 park rangers from throughout California during a training session at West Valley College in the 1970s. At the time, Jim was a ranger in Yosemite. Jim is now retired but still educating park rangers. He trains Texas State park rangers and is a consultant to park agencies throughout the world.

The Four "P's" of Protection

The highest priority of a park ranger, and the first "P," is to **protect people from other people**. This, of course, is the law enforcement part of his/her job. That part of the ranger job has never changed. A ranger's job has always been to protect. Crimes like stealing, assaults, abuse of alcohol, domestic disturbances, and driving too fast, unfor-

---

[68] Missouri State Parks website http://www.mostateparks.com.

tunately do occur in parks. Most weekends, a place like Yosemite National Park is a small mobile city. Most rangers today feel that crime has risen in their parks and is of great concern. In my experience, most issues I had to deal with were crimes against the park resource, like camping outside the campground and highway offenses like speeding. I had no room for using the lowest level when dealing with a speeder. I had picked too many bodies off the highway not to know the dangers of driving too fast in a park environment. I did have to make a couple of arrests of people wanted for felonies.

I had always been taught, however, to use the lowest effective enforcement level when it was possible to do so. Perhaps making a friend for the park and the profession might be more important than a citation for something where the person can be educated and released. Retired California State Park Ranger David Carle has said that administration and rangers needed to know that park law enforcement is just a little different.[69]

People who visit parks are usually on vacation and are there to have a good time. Some get in trouble because they do not know the proper outdoor manners when they use the park. Usually these people can be educated and let go with a warning. Of course, there are some people, like drug dealers and other crooks, who cannot be educated, and a higher enforcement level needs to take place. I feel strongly that rangers' attitudes have changed and that they are not using an "approachable" level anymore. It could be that the ranger's job really has not changed; the rangers have!

The second "P" is to **protect the people from the park**. Parks like Yosemite can be dangerous. Most people who visit parks are out of their urban element. Water runs fast, it snows sometimes in July or August, waterfalls are high, water flowing over granite can be slippery, rocks can hurt when you fall off of them, people from other countries are driving in rented cars and RVs, and bears (and raccoons in our local county parks) like to eat your food. In this modern age where most are not able to feel the pulse of the outdoors, people need help navi-

---

[69] David Carle, personal email to author, July 2006.

gating in a different environment than they are used to. This becomes more important in large natural areas everywhere, whether administered by the municipality, county, regional authorities, state, or national organizations.

The third "P" is the **protection of people from themselves**. Not having a basic knowledge of the outdoors, some park visitors sometimes do dangerous things and the park strikes back at them. Sometimes the result is lethal. Some visitors wade in the water above waterfalls or climb over protective barriers, like what happened at Yosemite's Vernal Falls in 2011. Three people were swept over the falls when they climbed over the barrier to have a picture taken. In a June 2013 incident, a young man was swimming above the falls and got swept away. Some visitors even try to hand feed a bear a potato chip, (most people wouldn't try that through the bars of a cage!) or try to go off trails without a compass or a map when hiking in unfamiliar places. People often are poorly prepared, physically or equipment-wise, for the environment. They bring their urban lifestyle into parks. To illustrate this lifestyle, Yosemite was having a problem with people in RVs pulling into turnouts to spend the night and not using the campgrounds. Before going off duty one evening, I made one last drive through the district. I found a van parked in the Olmsted Point turnout. When I approached the vehicle, the man inside said, "Yeah, I know I am not supposed to stay here but I am watching a TV program and this is the best place to get reception. I'll leave when the program is over."

California State Parks report that the most citations given in campgrounds were for undue noise. People forget that there are people who want to sleep. I remember a character I met on the trail one day at Gravelly Ford in the south end of Yosemite. He had on Bermuda shorts and tennis shoes, wore a pith helmet and a day pack, carried a sleeping bag under his arm, and was trying to use the map that was given to people at the entrance stations of the park as a trail guide. I shook my head. It appeared to be an accident about to happen. I didn't run into him again. I hope he isn't still out there.

The first three P's dealt with public safety. The fourth and last "P" is one of the primary reasons for having rangers. It is to **protect the park and the park resources from the people** so future generations will have nature to enjoy. It is one of the major functions of a park ranger to make sure that our parks and their resources are there for our grandchildren and for generations yet unborn. It is a very important "P" in the four "P's" of protection. A thirty-eight-year veteran of the California State Parks, Miles Standish, has said, "If the parks were to disappear tomorrow, there would be no reason to have rangers." How right he is. It is the reason we exist. Almost every ranger in my surveys listed this as the highest priority.

The Ranger and Resource Management: Protecting the Park

Protecting the park resources is in almost every ranger's job description. Even when they are specialists and resource management is not a part of their jobs, rangers still need to be the eyes and ears of park protection. It is the one thing that the public expects a ranger to be: a park protector. In order to be the eyes and ears of protection, they should at least know what they are looking at. Educating the visitor when that person has violated a rule connected to natural resources is the ideal time to use the lowest level of enforcement. Even if that person receives a notice of a violation in whatever form, they should walk away knowing the reasons for the rule and why it is important to the park to have such a regulation. For example, a person receiving a violation for letting a bear get their food in a campground should know why it is important to not let that happen. It is bad for the bear. They get used to human food and sometimes become destructive in their efforts to retrieve it. Almost every law enforcement contact can be an interpretive one.

Knowing the environment that you are working in is an important function of a park ranger. It is part of the "ranger image." Each ranger should have some basic knowledge of vegetation and wildlife management, how to recognize invasive plants and feral animals that are a problem to managing the resource, and what is of interest to a park visitor in their parks. Remember that it is easier to make an enforcement officer out of a ranger than the other way around. College courses in natural history should be required for every park position. Agencies should return to the standard of hiring people with other than Administration of Justice degrees, and annual training should be required in resource management. Like making a bad arrest can affect a person's life, bad resource management can have a huge effect on the park's resources for years to come.

Resource management is becoming very complex and that causes agencies to veer away from traditional roles for rangers into resource management specialists.

Wildland and Structural Fire Control and Management

In this specialized world, most wildland fires are fought by highly trained park fire crews. Both structural and wildland fire protection in most large national parks are handled that way. The East Bay Regional Park District has its own fire department, which is rare for a regional park system. Yosemite did as well. Since most rangers are usually the first on the scene for small wildland fires, they do know how to make the initial attack, how to evacuate visitors, and hopefully how to keep themselves out of trouble.

In Santa Clara County, each park unit has at least one pumper unit in a pickup bed and the rangers are trained on how to use it.

In Tuolumne we had training in structural fire and had full "turn out equipment," that included fireman hats, protective coats, pants, and boots. During my time in Yosemite, we got called out for such things as dumpster fires and tent cabin fires. Some people liked to put their hot charcoal in the dumpsters. We also had a couple of RV fires and auto fires, and the fire truck often rolled to the scene of auto accidents. I was the first on scene for three fires. One fire was started by an out-of-bounds camper in Tuolumne Meadows, and two campfires in the backcountry were not extinguished properly. In the old days, rangers would have had to camp by the fire until relieved. I just had to wait until the fire crew got there.

Santa Clara County Park prescribed fire in
Joseph Grant County Park (Photo by Don Rocha)

In the National Park Service, many rangers were certified in fire control and often were called out to fight fires all over the United States, meaning they were often out of their home parks for weeks. Being qualified to fight fire was a great, but dangerous, way to earn extra income. Fighting fire has since been taken away from protection rangers.

In a large park like Yosemite, fires started in a natural way (by lightning) above 8000 feet were allowed to burn. The fuel loads above that altitude were such that we could allow that to happen. I had two lightning fires in my backcountry area that burned for several weeks. Nature took care of one after a few weeks (rain) and the other was producing so much smoke in Yosemite Valley that the park fire control personnel put it out. Most rangers in national, state, and regional parks do get involved in helping with prescribed burns. Santa Clara County in the San Francisco Bay Area has a prescribed fire program that some rangers volunteer for, as do the California State Parks and other parks in the vicinity.

Search and Rescue

Park rangers save people from the park and from themselves. Some parks can be very dangerous places. Wet rocks can be slippery. The cliffs are sometimes steep, and unprepared people can get lost easily if they leave the trail. Urban people in an unfamiliar environment can cause problems. In most large national, state, and regional parks, a portion of what a ranger does is search and rescue (SAR). Rangers need to be trained and are constantly on call in emergencies, as not a day goes by without some incident that requires a ranger's assistance. It happens so often that there is an expert search and rescue ranger in Yosemite Valley whose job is to coordinate SAR events.

Every summer that I worked in Yosemite, there were at least a dozen incidents where climbers got into trouble or there was a major search for a lost person. Rangers in Tuolumne Meadows often trained in rock rescue. Rock climbing is "risk recreation" at its best. Risk recreation is an activity where the individual participating is at risk of bodily harm or even death. When a rock climber experiences a problem and needs to be rescued, the people involved in that rescue are also put at risk. If it requires the use of a helicopter, then those people face danger.

Dealing with death is a common occurrence in a place like Yosemite. One summer when I worked in Tuolumne Meadows, we had eleven deaths due to accidents, strokes, and other health issues. Four of those deaths were caused by an airplane crash.

Two seasonal rangers (Fred Koegler and I) were trained in conducting the search function. Fred volunteered in the off season for a search team in Los Angeles. I was a National Association of Search and Rescue course coordinator and taught the subject at West Valley College.

Most lost people do find themselves, but on occasion there is an all-out search for someone. This is true in most large open spaces in America. Fred had been on so many searches in Tuolumne Meadows that he knew where to expect those people to appear and how the terrain funnels people who are lost.

Tuolumne Meadows sub-district ranger Tom Habecker
giving a morning briefing for a search.
Author is standing by the tree in the background.
(Photo by Tom Habecker)

The picture above of a mixture of national park people and volunteers was taken during a search for a lost person that went on for over nine days and cost thousands of dollars without any success or even finding a clue. The case is still open.

Emergency Medical Services

Being a public servant requires rangers to be trained in some level of first aid and CPR. Every ranger job description I have ever read has had that as a requirement. Usually a person already has had first aid training when they are first hired. Agencies sometimes provide the updates, however.

Tom Habecker at the scene of an accident in the backcountry
in Yosemite. Tom is wearing protective equipment
that is required when flying in a helicopter.
(Photo by Tom Habecker)

Most of the permanent staff in Yosemite were trained as "park med-ics," which was similar to being a paramedic. Tom Habecker had spe-cial training on the heart monitor, and could give an IV. Although on-ly having to complete the Red Cross Advanced First Aid course, most of the seasonal protection rangers in Tuolumne were Emergency Medical Technicians (EMT). I was an EMT and got trained in the off season at my own expense. What I did as a ranger and the isolation that was Tuolumne Meadows almost required it.

We were 55 miles by road from the clinic. The park helicopter was only about twenty minutes away, but the rescue people from Lamore Naval Air Station were almost an hour away. The Tuolumne ambulance was parked in front of my tent cabin, and I was in it often. Honestly, the medical part of the job was tough for me to handle sometimes. I did not relish putting people in body bags or picking them up off the highway.

The Interpretive
Ranger/Naturalist/Historian/Educator

In 1871, John Muir, while living in Yosemite Valley, recorded in his notebook "I'll interpret the rocks, learn the language of flood, storm, and the avalanche. I'll acquaint myself with the glaciers and the wild gardens, and get as near to the heart of the world as I can."[70] It is believed that this was the first time that the word "interpret" was used in this sense. Muir, of course, wrote eloquently about Yosemite and what was found there in the natural world. Interpretation became the word used everywhere for the educational arm of every agency. Some rangers became "interpretive naturalists" or "ranger historians." They gave nature and history walks and talks, campfire programs, designed self-guided trails and bulletin boards, and presented living history programs. Some interested members of the early Cavalry troops that patrolled Yosemite and Yellowstone and other early parks started giving talks to visitors, mainly because they were always being asked about "what that flower is," or "can you tell us about those weird rock formations?" A nature museum was actually started by the Cavalry in Yosemite Valley, which exhibited a display of plants and animals in the administration building.

Prior to the beginning of organized interpretive programs, the custodian of the Casa Grande Ruins outside Phoenix, Arizona, started a display of Native American relics that became the first National Park Service exhibit. A year before, 1st Lt. Henry Pipes, a surgeon with the Cavalry, started an arboretum in Yosemite's Wawona District and had labeled plants along a path.

In the summer of 1919, National Park Service Director Steven Mather observed a nature walk at California's Lake Tahoe. Mr. Mather was very impressed by what he saw. He learned that the program and other naturalist activities were being financed by Dr. and Mrs. C.M. Goethe. Excited by what he saw, he talked to the Goethes, as well as two other members of his group, Dr. Harold Bryant and Dr. Loye Mil-

---

[70] National Park Service, http://www.nps.gov.

ler, into taking the programs to Yosemite National Park. A considerable amount of the financing came from Mather's own pocket, although the Goethes shared expenses. This initiative became the beginning of a division of parks with employees specifically hired to educate the public about what was around them and how to get the most enjoyment out of their park visit.

Now many agencies have interpretive functions in their parks, delivered by a variety of ways and means. Campfire talks, slide shows, self-guided nature trails and guided walks appeared. The traditional ranger, who did "all of the above," and specialists in history, geology, and native plants and animals, were hired. If an agency is short on staff, docents (volunteer) programs were started using the expertise outside the park community. Biology, science, and history teachers often were used. They were hired during the busy seasons, usually in the summer. Some rangers chose to transfer to that division of park management and get out of being an enforcement ranger. Over the years, the National Park Service has become a leader in professional interpretive programming and planning, with an interpretive training center in Harper's Ferry, Virginia. The State of California's rangers all go to the Mott Training Center at Asilomar for interpretive training.

Interpretive rangers can be important in changing attitudes of park visitors and in explaining and promoting the whys and wherefores of park agency rules and regulations. When a problem occurred in Yosemite from people breaking into vehicles to steal what was there, the mention of that at campfire programs educated the public and helped stem the problem. Asking people to cooperate with the park service to control the bear problem by not leaving their food out and unprotected was a lead-in to virtually every interpretive program for several years. As a protection ranger, I personally felt I was as much an interpreter as those whose job that was.

As a mounted ranger, I was far more visible and approachable than a ranger in a patrol vehicle. As Chief Ranger Bill Wendt told me once, "You cannot pet a patrol car." A very large number of my daily contacts with people were interpretive in nature. When I was in a patrol car, most contacts I had were in conflict situations, and I really had very few of those over the course of a day, usually less than ten. As a horse patrolman, I sometimes had over 200 contacts in any given day.

Santa Clara County interpreter giving a talk in Almaden/Quicksilver Park. (Photo by the author)

Many regional park systems also hired excellent and devoted interpreters. The East Bay Regional Park District that encompasses two counties in San Francisco Bay's East Bay has one of the best naturalist programs in the world. My own county park department in the Silicon Valley of California has a budding interpretive program that has great potential in a system with many diverse natural parks that range from sea level to over 2000 feet in elevation and has vegetation from cattails on the edge of San Francisco Bay to redwood forests in the Santa Cruz Mountains. It also has historic sites important to the county. With the new generation of people, more tuned to the urban environment coming into the professional ranger ranks, it is really important that good interpretive training is available to every new park ranger.

While the job of ranger has not changed much over the years, society as a whole has, and the emphasis on enforcement has increased. The issues facing parks that were discussed in Section 1 of this book have had an impact on rangers: how they do their jobs, their backgrounds, and their attitudes. A number of landmark events have changed the landscape of the ranger job.

Section 3
Park Rangers and the
Challenges of the Modern World

A 1976 self-defense training class with James T. Reynolds and Jim Brady, both NPS rangers. Photo was taken in the WVC Wrestling room at an in-service training session. (Photo: West Valley College)

Chapter 10: The Turning Point for the Ranger's Role

The Stoneman Meadow Incident

The country was in upheaval in the 1960s and 1970s. Among the nation's youngest adult members, the "Age of Aquarius" and peace and love of the 1960s turned into violent protests against the Vietnam War and against authority. In my own early high school and college years of the fifties, I had seen the first signs of protests about war and "police actions" like what was going on in Korea. No one wanted to go fight that war. The meltdown of society was not just over war. There were plenty of other things to worry about, like a deep economic recession, and the beginning of terrorism when the Palestinian Liberation Organization killed 11 Israeli athletes at the 1972 Munich Olympic Games. In the face of stress, people sought freedom.

Young people, mostly of college age, flocked to places like national parks and even local and state parks. Parks were places where they thought they could have the freedom to gather and do whatever they wanted to do.

On Memorial Day weekend in 1970, Yosemite Valley experienced a large influx of young visitors from the San Francisco Bay Area. Theft and the use of drugs in the park increased. Many arrests were made and rangers had to work long hours to control the situation. That was a major hint that the Park had some trouble brewing for the coming summer.[71] The counterculture of the Vietnam War was at its peak, and these young people chose parks to show their enthusiasm for free speech and contempt for authority.[72]

On July 4, 1970, a catalytic event changed the course of parks and ranger programs in this country. A large group of young people in the counterculture gathered in the Stoneman Meadow in Yosemite Valley to have a party. Being in that meadow off-trail was not against the

---

[71] Farabee, op. cit. p. 125
[72] Morris, op. cit.

law, but the large crowds were causing much ecological damage. As that weekend grew longer, the crowds became larger. The news had traveled fast. It was circulated around the country that Yosemite was "wide open" to such an activity. Individuals began foraging through the campgrounds, stealing camping equipment and even food off of tables as people sat eating. Sleeping bags and other items were stolen from right under the noses of families and other park visitors. There were reports of fornicating along park side roads, vandalism, the destruction of park property, drinking, and drug use. There were also reports that guns might be present in the meadow.

Using interpretive naturalists, the National Park Service attempted to reason with the group, asking them to leave the meadow, and telling them about the environmental damage that was taking place. The attempt to educate them did not work. They did not care about environmental issues or the damage they were causing. A riot ensued when the Park decided that the people should be forcibly removed. Rangers gave them a deadline to leave and then attempted to sweep through the meadow with mounted rangers and wranglers from Curry Company (the private concession operator) on untrained horses, along with other rangers and maintenance workers on foot, when the deadline was not met. Outside help appeared from local law enforcement agencies. Many people were arrested.

It was not the proudest moment in National Park Service history. It did open some eyes very wide as to the Service's inability to deal with modern society in a law enforcement sense with untrained people with degrees in Forestry or Parks and Recreation.

After the riot, Yosemite ranger Lee Shackleton and rangers from other parks in the system were summoned before Congress to explain why the Congressional mandate to "promote and regulate" in the 1916 Act creating the national parks had been ignored. After a major General Accounting Office investigation into growing crime in the outdoor recreation areas of the Federal Government, Congress was concerned about the rank amateur response by rangers.[73]

---

[73] Personal email communication from Lee Shackleton, July 6th 2006.

Congress told Lee that he and other rangers had to go back to their respective parks and tell everyone that the Organic Act of 1916 was a direction from Congress and that the visitors who came to their parks had to be provided the same level of professional law enforcement protection as they had come to expect back home in their own communities. The Park Service also received a threat that if they didn't provide it, Congress would! Congress threatened to enlist a national police force to provide protection to the parks if the rangers did not.

The Park Service reacted by sending their park rangers to be trained at the National Park Police Academy in Washington, D.C. Most of the seasonal rangers were grandfathered into their summer positions. I had been in the Military Police when in the Army, and that helped me get through this screening but eventually I took leave from the college where I was teaching to attend an enforcement academy in Santa Rosa, California. Lee also said that in his opinion, during the time that he was Yosemite's Chief Law Enforcement Officer, the worst arrests, citations, and evidentiary chains of custody were created by the best ranger generalists.[74] It appeared to Lee that specialists were needed and not generalists.

The Law Enforcement Bandwagon

After the riot of July 1970, the emphasis on rangers better trained in law enforcement began. Agencies everywhere in the country changed their training regimes. Permanent rangers went to "Pig School" at the National Park Police Academy in Washington, D.C., and "Pine Pig" tee shirts appeared on off-duty rangers.

The General Authorities Act was enacted in 1976, six years after the riot, and it really changed what national park rangers were able to do. The Act authorized national park rangers to openly carry firearms and make arrests without warrant, to execute a warrant issued by the court and to conduct investigations of offenses committed in the Na-

---

[74] Op. cit.

tional Park System.[75] This Act made park rangers the same as any law enforcement person in the country. The Authorities Act required 40 hours of law enforcement update every year. Every ranger became a commissioned law enforcement officer. Permanent rangers became "FLETC" trained at the Federal Law Enforcement Training Center in Glenco, Georgia. It is a practice still in place today. FLETC is a 20-week program that covers law, defensive tactics, search and rescue, first aid, and defensive and pursuit driving.

The California State Parks soon followed suit. A 1968 report produced by the California Peace Officers Standards and Training (POST) Commission laid out the facts about increased crime in the state parks and the inability of State Parks to satisfactorily guarantee the safety of visitors to its parks. The director, Bill Mott, only had two viable choices: keep the function in-house or contract with outside agencies to do the law enforcement job. To keep a "park face" on the enforcement, the decision was made to add state park rangers to the list of peace officers and properly equip and train them for the job of law enforcement at California State Park Training Center.[76]

After the Yosemite riot, there was a "tri-agency" conference called in Yosemite that included the United States Forest Service, Yosemite, and the California State Parks. The State had had several thousand recorded felonies in their large park system and was receiving pressure from local enforcement agencies to "take care of their own enforcement problems."[77]

Employees of the California State Parks who were hired in the early '70s were not yet peace officers and were not authorized to carry a firearm. At that time, rangers in the State Parks needed to have a four year degree in either the natural sciences or history to qualify for em-

---

[75] *Director's Order #9: Law Enforcement Program*, approved by NPS Director Fran Maindella, March 23, 2006.
[76] Jeff Price, retired California State Park Ranger, personal email communication, July 2006.
[77] Dana Long, retired California State Park Ranger, personal email communication, July 2006.

ployment. This requirement was lifted so they could hire enforcement people and affirmative action employees.

Park agencies everywhere started to jump on the law enforcement bandwagon. The City of Santa Ana, in Southern California, hired 12 part-time rangers to patrol their parks. A local park director in Los Gatos, a small community in the San Francisco Bay Area, was approached by the chief of police and told that he did not want to have to have to deal with problems in parks and that the director ought to consider hiring park rangers. He had been to a meeting of police chiefs about crime problems in parks, and arming county park rangers. Los Gatos hired four. The city of San Jose had already started a ranger program because of pressure from the city police to monitor and take care of their own problems.

Santa Clara County was also not immune to park enforcement problems. Parts of both regional and local parks were "taken over" by people who were there to create trouble. Stevens Creek, Hellyer County Parks, and the city's Alum Rock City Park became places where you would think twice before taking your family for a picnic. The rangers in our local county Parks and Recreation department went before the Board of Supervisors and won the right to become armed. The city of San Jose was also seeing a rise in crime and had more incidents in a month than the county had in one year. The San Jose rangers are still not full peace officers (armed) but have had full Peace Officer Standards and Training (POST).

To Arm or Not to Arm?

After the Yosemite incident people in the park management seats had trouble accepting the new thrust toward arming rangers and giving them more enforcement authority. Some lobbied not to go in that direction, because it was not the image of a park ranger as perceived by the public, but by park administration. Most were "old guard" employees. Most were those generalist rangers who had come up through the ranks and firmly believed that arming rangers would soil the "good guy" image that had been fostered over the years. The

160

same attitudes prevailed with other administrators in park agencies everywhere. When they caved to the pressure and the rangers were given the responsibility to carry arms again, the progression went through several steps:

> "Okay, but keep them in the ranger station or locked in your vehicle."

> "Keep them in your briefcase so they would not be seen."

> "Carry them on your person where they will not be seen."

> "Wear full police leather: show them you are armed."

When rangers were first allowed to carry arms in Yosemite, they carried small weapons in a holster under their coat and around their backside where they would not be obvious. They were small five-shot chief specials. The spare rounds I had were carried loosely in my pocket. I had trouble hitting the wall of a building with that weapon and ended up buying my own, a 38 caliber Smith and Wesson. Now most park agencies that arm their rangers have them in full police leather. Supervisors feared the reaction of the public when this happened. In the course of my NPS career that covered 15 summers, I had only been asked once about my weapon. Not "why," but "how long" had rangers been armed? I had to tell him that rangers have been armed as long as there have been National Park Service rangers.

I found myself right in the middle of the argument between the Santa Clara County Parks Department that was advocating for arming rangers and the County Executive and the Board of Supervisors that were arguing against it. The rangers leaned on me for support, which I freely gave. I believe that they turned to me because I had provided in-service training to them every year. The title of our most popular training session was "The Ranger Without Weapons." That in-service training was taught by National Park Service instructors who were now armed and more like specialists than generalists. I guess that I unwittingly became a big part of changing attitudes.

I ended up in the Santa Clara County administrator's office one day with the police chiefs from all the surrounding cities, along with the county sheriff and the county park director. The director had written a "law enforcement procedure" document that he wanted to present to this group and a part of that was supporting the training and arming of the local county rangers. All of a sudden, I was the expert and very much in the hot seat. The chiefs ganged up on me. They did not support the idea at all! However, the end result was that law enforcement training at our local police academy and the carrying of weapons did follow for the rangers. The incidents of violence directed toward rangers have all but disappeared.

After a year or two, the weapons were taken away from the county rangers. The county sheriff didn't like two law enforcement agencies in his county, and the sheriff had more political power. There were also some incidents of high speed chases in parks and other questionable reactions by county rangers to several enforcement situations.

After the rangers had their weapons taken away, the Santa Clara County Parks Department then enlisted the help of the sheriff by creating a "park patrol" composed of sheriff's deputies at a cost that was then a million dollars a year! In my opinion, it was the sheriff's way of getting more money and I thought that this answer only partially worked. As retired NPS Superintendent Doug Morris puts it, "It is easier to make a law enforcement officer out of a park ranger, than a ranger out of a law enforcement officer." The sheriff deputies had no interest in asking people to leash their dogs.

The county sheriff soon called me to tell me that he wanted our college to train these individuals. He said, "Don't worry, we'll give you people that are outdoor oriented." My answer was that was "probably true, but being 'outdoor oriented' to them meant high power hunting rifles and off road vehicles." There was a silence, then a chuckle, and he said, "I guess you are right about that!"

The first hour of this training covered what a park was and the reasons why we need to protect them. I have since met several times, usually over lunch, with the sheriff's park supervisor to talk about the same subject. The last time I did this it was a lot easier because the new supervisor was once a park ranger and he knew the importance of what I was telling him.

The deputies still had little interest in policing park resource management problems caused by visitors. Damage to a hillside by a four-wheel drive vehicle caught in the act was "no big deal" to a deputy. To a ranger, it was a big deal! It cost hundreds of dollars to repair. There was also a problem with just keeping the Sheriff Park Unit in the park. There was not enough "action," and they were willingly called out of parks to back up other patrol units or to find action elsewhere.

The East Bay Regional Park District (EBRPD), one of the largest regional park districts in the nation, covers Alameda and Contra Costa Counties in the San Francisco Bay Area. The EBRPD turned over their enforcement duties to a public safety division within their park system. This was a full police department with a chief, helicopters, and all the trimmings. The change happened when the system they had in place (untrained park rangers) didn't seem to work in the face of climbing crime rates in parks. The rangers in EBRPD now do maintenance, provide resource management, and give citations for local ordinances that pertain to park resources. EBRPD has its own tax base, and money is usually available for such a structure. Santa Clara County must share tax revenues.

The EBRPD has a wonderful naturalist division as part of their calling. Some of the best interpreters in the United States are on their staff. It is certainly a grand example of using specialization in their organization, and I might have to agree that this could be the way to go. Perhaps if Santa Clara County had gone this route, the rangers would have kept their full peace officer status. To have the state pay for the training, you have to have an organizational structure like that of a police department which would not be that hard to do. Why not offer a position under control of the Sheriff's Department to park rangers. The Park Forward Commission for California State Parks also has recommended that the state take a hard look at establishing a separate law enforcement position.

Ranger Safety

One of the 4 P's of protection deals with keeping people safe from other people. I have said little about ranger safety. The murder of Ken Patrick at Point Reyes discussed later in this book was another wakeup call. Providing safety equipment to the park ranger has been the crux of the issue over specialization. Being a law enforcement officer, no matter who you work for or where you are working, is not the safest job in the world. Dealing with people in conflict is dangerous. In some parks, the enforcement ranger is often a long way from any backup help. A former student who transferred from state parks to the highway patrol told me that he felt much safer patrolling the freeways than when he was a ranger because of the isolation. It takes only a very few minutes to get someone by your side when you are a highway patrolman, but it takes 15-20 minutes or more to get help in state parks or in a regional system.

It probably is only a matter of time before other agencies experience what happened to Ken Patrick. In 1977, the Army Corps of Engineers ranger Opal James was shot and killed in an incident in Arkansas. I have a friend in the Sacramento County Parks who took several bullets into his armored vest from a drug dealer he was chasing on foot. Even though park rangers in Santa Clara County are often confronted by dangerous people, they are only provided vests and pepper spray.

Park rangers all over the world have been murdered in the line of duty. In the National Park Service, nine such incidents have occurred. The first three were National Park Police, one as far back as 1927 at Hot Springs, Arkansas. However, the last six deaths were rangers on duty in our national parks. After Ranger Ken Patrick's death in Point Reyes in 1973, five more have paid the ultimate price in places like Gulf Islands, Great Smokies, Organ Pipe, Kaloko-Honokohau, and recently in Mount Rainer National Park in 2012. All of the above were trained law enforcement officers, armed and with full peace powers.

Other incidents have taken the lives of rangers and other employees in parks. As in any profession that places a person in a position of peril, rangers have died in auto accidents, fires, and rescues. I often felt that riding a horse on granite and slick rock was not the safest thing to do.

The National Park Service Ranger Futures Study

Retired NPS Superintendent Douglas Morris relates how the Congress, the Department of Interior (DOI), and the NPS all responded decisively to what was happening in our national parks. Congress held hearings. The director of NPS, George Hartzog, ordered all rangers to be trained. Interior issued, for the first time, a comprehensive Law Enforcement Policy. In 1975 NPS also issued NPS-9, a set of enforcement guidelines that have since been revised and updated over time. In 1980 there was an approval for all rangers to carry a firearm when carrying out law enforcement duties.[78]

Changes in the 1970s that resulted in a more professional law enforcement approach worried the champions of the traditional ranger role.

In 1976 a "Ranger Image Task Force" was created to study the concerns brought forth about the loss of the traditional ranger image. Specialization had a huge part in the evolution of the ranger at this point. The NPS also tried to divide the duties of the ranger between a more "professional" park ranger and a "technician." The professional rangers were supposed to have more knowledge than the technicians and were expected to transfer and move up within the system.[79] They also were higher in rank in the governmental pay system. The technicians were supposed to be local people not interested in moving around. It didn't work out that way. The people in hiring positions were able to pick out the best candidates, and those were people just as highly educated as they were and took those positions to get a more permanent job in NPS. It did not take long for highly educated technicians to become dissatisfied with not being able to move up in

---

[78] Douglas Morris, "Professional Opinion Paper- Reviewing the Park Ranger Profession, Coalition of National Park Service Retirees," Year unknown.
[79] Morris, op. cit.

the system. This led to another effort to find a solution to this problem.

A new comprehensive initiative was created in the spring of 1992 called the "Ranger Futures Working Group" and then later labeled "Ranger Careers."[80] The goal of this initiative was to upgrade the position of park ranger to a higher level. Job descriptions for all levels were changed to include "knowledge of natural and/or cultural resources" and contained language that allowed law enforcement rangers higher pay and retirement benefits. The higher pay rate was needed because rangers were leaving the profession for jobs in municipal police and state highway patrol units as well as the Bureau of Land Management and other units within the Department of Interior. The rangers wanted to get paid for what they did and to enjoy a comfortable retirement. These changes also had a huge effect on the budgets of parks and caused a lot of people to remain in enforcement and not move up into supervisory positions because of the benefits that went with being in law enforcement, like early retirement.

It was found that NPS was experiencing a 25% turnover among graded park rangers who were leaving for better jobs and benefits. It was calculated that each ranger who left the agency after serving only two years cost NPS $250,000 in training, experience, and administrative and management costs.[81]

As was the case when the Park Rangers Association of California began when they could not define what a ranger was, the Rangers Futures Group was finding out that they could not describe exactly what their own rangers did. There appeared to be a large difference in what a ranger's responsibilities were within different NPS units in the system. Some were doing only protection, some had resource management responsibilities, some rangers gave interpretive talks, and some

[80] Morris, op. cit.
[81] Brady, James, "A Brief History of the Ranger Careers Initiative in the National Park Service," A Congressional, Interior Department and NPS Summary Paper of the Ranger Futures Working Group. (This paper also was sent to all the park superintendents so that they were aware of what was happening with the group.) 1994-95.

backcountry people were even doing maintenance. To complicate matters, the job of park ranger work did not fall neatly into any occupational group or job designated by the U.S. Office of Personnel Management (OPM).[82]

Historically rangers came from different educational backgrounds. Some came to the profession with a degree from a four-year college and some had only a high school diploma. All performed all types of work within the agency, from field level ranger duties to technical and administrative duties. On top of that, there were no specific educational requirements for the position of park ranger. OPM placed the ranger in the "miscellaneous occupations group." There appears to be no specific four-year educational program available in this country that trains just park rangers. You cannot get a degree in just being a park ranger. Thus the ranger "profession," by definition, is not really a profession.

The 1991 "Vail Agenda" specifically called for a degree requirement for park rangers. The Vail Agenda came from the National Park Service's 75th Anniversary Symposium, which was held in Vail, Colorado. Attending were top managers, along with distinguished government, academic, and private leaders who examined almost every major aspect of park operations and management.[83]

The following were key Vail Agenda findings regarding park rangers:

- Rangers must be versatile, adaptable, and able to independently integrate a broad variety of information in complex field settings and their decisions have far-reaching consequences.

- The park ranger series should have a degree requirement at entry level. Degrees could be in either natural resources or cultural resources/history specialties. There should be a specific list of qualifying degrees.

---

[82] Op. cit.
[83] Op. cit.

167

- Recommendations were made requiring training, development, and management.[84]

Taking all into consideration, the Ranger Futures Working Group produced their Ranger of the Future Concept Paper in 1994. A few of the accomplishments were as follows:

- Created service-wide position descriptions for all park rangers.

- Developed new qualification standards for park rangers that included at least 24 units in natural or cultural sciences as minimal requirements.

- Enhanced annuity retirement coverage for law enforcement and fire fighting rangers.

- Developed new seasonal ranger position descriptions.

- Developed a new medical standard for law enforcement personnel.

- Developed a new field training program for enforcement rangers.

- Obtained increased appropriations.

- Set new physical fitness standards.

Park agencies all over the country were watching the result of this NPS working group with interest because the problems were almost the same everywhere. The California State Parks also created a Generalist Ranger Task Force, along with an impartial study committee, The Hoover Commission, to study this evolution. Although both suggested that the ranger retain the approachable "park culture" in their enforcement duties, they also made several suggestions as to how the state parks were to be managed in the future. They also considered the role of the park ranger in state parks, even suggesting that the state have both peace officers and generalists.

---

[84] Op. cit.

Yosemite had its own task force looking at what a ranger did. Because of the enforcement controversy that was a part of life in Yosemite, a Ranger Task Force was created in 1977 to define what a "traditional ranger" did in Yosemite. The task force was led by Gene Muehleisen, a National Park Service consultant and former director of California's Police Officer Standards and Training Academy (POST). Their results were as follows, with my comments in italics:

1. Visitor contact and interpretation. (*Interpretation in this sense would be just telling a visitor "what that tree is." I did do a living history program on the Cavalry and there were horse patrol rangers in Yosemite Valley who did formal programs about using horses.*)

2. Ability to communicate policy and regulations and safety procedures.

3. Wildlife protection. (*Yes, the bears did need protection! Eating human food was not good for them.*)

4. Prevention and spread of exotic plants and animals.

5. Inspection of sanitary conditions.

6. Fire and environmental conditions hazardous to public safety.

7. Administration of permit systems.

8. Management of campgrounds, beaches and picnic areas. (*Some rangers supervised fee collectors and campground managers.*)

9. Search and rescue operations.

10. Scuba diving. (*Usually a part of search and rescue*)

11. Use of saddle and pack stock.

12. Use of mechanized equipment. (*I had to use a loader when working in the corral.*)

13. Conducting investigations.

14. Arrest, search, and seizure.

15. Prevention of crime and violations.

16. Prevention of alcohol and drug abuse, alcohol violations and drug arrests.

17. Fee collections. (*Supervise entrance station personnel*)

18. Render first aid.

In addition, rangers write volumes of reports. A typical park ranger in my county does all of the above with the exception of criminal investigations. They once had a horse patrol unit, but no mule packing. Being a ranger is a complex job.

There is much to be done in parks besides enforcement, and many rangers agree that it is important to the survival of the parks that these functions continue.

Chapter 11: The Changing Role of Rangers

Enforcement emphasis for rangers is not a totally new stance taken by modern day rangers. Most park agencies, particularly county and municipal, cannot afford anything less than a ranger who can accomplish more than just enforcement. Their traditional or generalist rangers have been adept at handling more than just one job requirement, including enforcement. There is no better financial "bang for the buck" than a generalist ranger. The generalist ranger role has been an item for discussion for a very long time.

I was preparing my part of a panel presentation on this subject at the 2007 California Park Conference, when I ran across an old ranger journal from the Park Rangers Association of California. In this journal was a summary article about a similar panel that I had chaired at the 1977 California Park Conference, entitled, "The Specialist versus the Generalist." Thirty years later, I was preparing to participate in a panel on the very same subject! This article inspired me to poll people I knew, both retired and active in park management, to see what they thought about how the job of a park ranger had changed. Several things were cited, including the move toward greater law enforcement emphasis as an aftermath of the 1970 Yosemite riot, the changing society, and the unionization of park employees. The riot changed some views about how we managed the park visitors to keep them safe. The unions were started, for the most part, to make the rangers' lives safer and just a little easier, with shorter work days, better pay, and better equipment.

The consensus of the people polled was also that rangers are somehow different in this modern time, as are the people who are visiting the parks. Now the vast majority of the American public (80%) live in an urban area and there is an influx of people from foreign lands with different backgrounds and cultures visiting parks. Many now seem to lack even a vague idea about nature or what parks are all about, and why they have been set aside. Some park visitors do not see parks as places of beauty or of historical or cultural significance but rather as an outdoor gymnasium.

The rangers I queried felt that people who come into the park profession need to have a passion for protection of natural land values. That passion is usually gained from outdoor experiences and not from a classroom. The passion for nature seems to be less present in some modern-day rangers, and I feel the situation may get worse as people grow up in a more urban society.

The Stoneman Meadow Incident Increased the Ranger's Enforcement Role

The riot in Stoneman Meadow in Yosemite on July 4, 1970 was the event most often mentioned by old time national park rangers as the incident that changed the role of rangers to focus more on enforcement. Tom Habecker, a longtime employee of the National Park Service and once my Yosemite supervisor, said that the riot was the "watershed" event that changed things.[85] I feel that many modern day rangers probably do not even know about the Yosemite riot, as none mentioned it as the cause in a poll I conducted in 2013.

Santa Clara County had a small "riot" of its own in one of our local parks not long after the Stoneman Meadow incident. Large crowds gathered, rangers lost control, and the local police agencies had to be called in. As in Yosemite, there was drug use, crimes were being committed, and there was no respect for enforcement personnel. Also like Yosemite, the rangers and the local sheriff deputies were not trained to handle what was happening. The rangers had been told by the sheriff not to get involved. To add to the difficulty, local government officials were also on the scene, and the County Sheriff seemed to side with the rioters.

Bruce McKeeman, who worked in Yosemite from 1973 until 1981, agreed that the riots caused the National Park Service to see that there were people behaving illegally and in some instances preying upon the public. Bruce said that when he worked in the park, the Service started hiring seasonal rangers from police science programs, and he

---

[85] Thomas Habecker, email communication to the author, March 2007.

thought that was a disaster and one key to the deterioration of attitudes once found in the generalist ranger.[86] Other structures of government, like state, regional, and municipal park agencies acted in the same manner. They also leaned toward the hiring of people in police science.

Beside the riot, there was another event that happened that opened the eyes of National Park Service officials. August 5, 1973, a park ranger was shot and killed in Point Reyes National Seashore when he approached a suspect vehicle in a poaching incident. Ranger Ken Patrick's death was a shock to everyone. Ranger Patrick had wisely written the license plate number of the vehicle on a pad on the front seat of the patrol car, and the suspects were apprehended and punished. On January 1, 2012, Mount Rainier Ranger Margaret Anderson was murdered while attempting a road block to halt a subject that drove past a chain requirement sign without stopping. This was only one of several other incidents in national parks where rangers were shot and killed since the passing of Ranger Patrick.

Mandated Training

I have always told my students that a very high percentage of all park visitors are really very nice people. I called these statistics "Smitty's back pocket stats." The percentages were always based upon gut feelings. Of course, there were always a small percentage of people who got into trouble because they were not "tuned" to the right way of doing things in the outdoors. They'd wash their hair in the creek, feed the wildlife, or pick wildflowers. Of course, a minute percentage of visitors were there to commit serious crime. Because of that very small percentage, rangers had to be effectively trained to handle those criminal incidents. Law enforcement can affect lives for a long time; therefore, making the right decisions was important.

The modern ranger has to be trained well in a variety of skills and concepts as they pertain to the profession. One of those skills is that of

---

[86] Bruce McKennon, email communication to the author, March 2007.

a good and competent law enforcement officer. Because law enforcement could, and often does, affect the lives of people, a ranger must be trained pretty well. In the books about early rangers that I have read, there was no mention at all about enforcement training. I am sure they had to be aware of the laws at the time, and did their duty to enforce them.

My first year as a seasonal in Santa Clara County Parks, training was non-existent. "Read this, here are the patrol truck keys, go get 'em!" The reading material was a notebook of memos from the administration office that was used as a ranger manual. I also had to read a manual on how to put the truck into four-wheel drive and the book of park regulations. I did have a background in enforcement because I was a military policeman in the army. Not long after that, seasonal rangers for the county had to have a 40 hour course in arrest, search, and seizure.

As early as 1951, Yosemite rangers attended a National Park Police Academy in Washington D.C.[87] All full-time National Park Service rangers in the protection division now must attend the Federal Law Enforcement Training Academy (FLETC) in Glenco, Georgia. Seasonal rangers must also have a Federal Law Enforcement Commission if they are to enforce the law. They can usually get that by attending a special National Park Service Seasonal Enforcement Academy or other similar law enforcement academy.

When I was grandfathered into my position because of my experience and the fact that I had been in the military police, I had to document all my previous hours of enforcement training, experience (which included the eight weeks of military training and my old seasonal position with Santa Clara County Parks), and any other related training, before I was able to hold that first Federal Law Enforcement Commission. Later, I did go on sabbatical leave to attend the Criminal Justice Training Academy in Santa Rosa, California. I attended the special National Park Service Enforcement Academy for five weeks, which

---

[87] Shirley Sargent, *Protecting Paradise: Yosemite Rangers 1898-1960*, Ponderosa Press, Yosemite, California, 1998.

was two hundred hours. Eventually, I even taught at the Criminal Justice Training Academy for a day each session. That job offer came when I complained that the students should have some exposure to park enforcement and to park culture. The result was the job offer. You want to complain, you do it! So I did!

I taught conflict management and communication skills with a "park twist" for eight hours on a Friday in the middle of the Academy session. I used campgrounds and other sites in my scenarios. When I walked into the room and announced that I was a park ranger and that we were going to talk about parks, the class stood up and cheered! Literally! They were tired of being trained by police officers and sheriffs. My commute was over 200 miles round trip, but I took on the challenge because I was sold on the traditional backgrounds and attitudes needed for park rangers. My evaluations for the day's training were always filled with statements that it was about time park rangers appeared.

Bill Orr, from the Western Regional Office of the National Park Service, soon took over the running of the Academy, and he made many changes to keep the park face in all sessions of the training. The Academy now has a "model" campground for enforcement scenarios named after Bill, who has since passed away. Former Yosemite Ranger Lee Shackleton also ended up teaching there after he retired, as did other National Park employees. Santa Rosa was the first such NPS Academy, but soon this concept spread over the United States, and it was offered other places as well.

California State Parks created their own Enforcement Academy at the William Penn Mott Training Center at Asilomar near Monterey, California. Bill Mott was a California park icon and ended his career as the director of the National Park Service during the Reagan Administration. Bill was State Park director during Reagan's governorship of California and a former director of East Bay Regional Park District. The training center was created because Bill wanted to put a "park face" on enforcement. The California state park ranger training that takes place is certified by the California Police Officers and Standards Training (POST) commission. Their academy is now at Butte College

175

in Redding. Many other park agencies throughout California also use POST certified training and other park agencies in states in the U.S. also use such training for their park rangers.

Every year, laws change, or new laws are brought into the system. Park rangers, like all enforcement officers, need to have their resume updated and have to qualify with their service weapon. In fact, the Federal 1976 General Authorities Act mandated such training for National Park Service rangers. Under that act, all rangers have to go through forty hours of updated instruction each year. Updates were always a part of the training we held at West Valley College, particularly the search and seizure changes that seem to happen annually because of court cases. Being a law enforcement officer becomes a matter of liability. You need to go through updates and continue to qualify often with your service weapon. Both training and qualifying with a weapon took time away from duty, sometimes leaving the park without sufficient people to run the facilities.

In Yosemite, this training was usually done the week before we reported for patrol duty. You could also get it by attending class during the winter. Housing in Yosemite Valley, where the training was held, was nonexistent. It was a fifty-five mile commute from Tuolumne to the Yosemite Valley. One spring, when the training was held during school spring vacation, I even rented an RV to live in. That did not go over well with my wife, but it did provide me some empathy for the RV owners who used our park roads. I had been there, done that!

By the time our careers were over, we had well over a thousand hours of law enforcement training. Some of my friends in other areas of park management longed to have the same training mandate in their areas of expertise, like resource management. Tom Habecker suggests that any park enforcement training should also cover the "culture of parks and the foundations that gave us our jobs and the national parks." I could not agree more.

Changing Training Requirements

Before 1990, new employees in the ranger ranks in the National Park Service were asked to attend a ranger skills class at the Horace Albright Training Center at the Grand Canyon. This ten-week class had a variety of subject matter taught by the experts and had a variety of people take advantage of that experience. My classmates included rangers, naturalists, a national park policeman, maintenance folks, and administrators. The operations course covered the management of large parks and recreation areas, historic sites, search and rescue, resource management, interpretation, a minimum amount of law enforcement, and maintenance. It also included several field trips so that the student could see problems first hand. Most importantly, it covered the history of the National Park Service, the key players in that agency's development, and the evolution of the Service's management philosophy. I took a sabbatical leave from the college to attend, and if other people got out of those ten weeks what I did, they spent the rest of their careers motivated like I was after it was over. Alas, there is no more ranger skills course for new intake rangers to attend.

The ranger skills class put a "park face" on what a ranger is supposed to be in the National Park Service. It taught everyone that there is more to park rangers than just law enforcement, and that we were all a part of a large family of public service employees. What I got out of it all was a great feeling of pride in working for the National Park Service and having the honor of wearing the grey and green and the flat hat. Now people are coming into the service without that introduction and that pride.

California State Park intake rangers (cadets) still attend the Mott Training Center at Asilomar, where the curriculum is similar to Albright's ranger skills program, which includes resource management, interpretation, and land management. However, they attend only after completing the enforcement academy. Training like this is an important first step to get back to where rangers are rangers. Other agencies should take note and follow that training sequence.

A training session involving a simulated automobile
accident in Tuolumne Meadows. The author is in the middle
of the road as incident commander. (Photo by Tom Habecker)

Doug Morris, a retired park superintendent from the National Park
Service and a former instructor at Albright, cites the removal of ranger skills from the Albright curriculum in 1990 as being one of the major causes of the specialist attitudes that rangers now seem to have.[88]
Lee Shackleton also bemoaned the loss of the ranger skills curriculum,
but feels that anyone motivated to be a ranger can, with the proper
validation and training, learn how to relocate a bear, fell a burning
snag with a crosscut, and speak to a violator in educational language.[89]

Jeff Price, a retired California state park ranger, believes that you do
not have to have a background based upon outdoor skills to be successful in the state system.[90] Some may disagree with Jeff and Lee.
Passion for the natural world and the motivation to protect it comes
from experience gained through exposure to the outdoors and not

[88] Douglas Morris, personal communication with the author, June 2007.
[89] Lee Shackleton, email correspondence to author dated July 6, 2006.
[90] Jeff Price, personal communication with the author, June 2006.

from a couple of training sessions or a college course. I would also agree that those who work in a very urban environment probably do not need to know how to survive in an adverse environment.

West Valley College's Park Management program, a Community College program located in Saratoga, California has a required outdoor skills class in the curriculum. The course was put there because the advisory committee to the program asked to have it put there. This advisory committee is made up of National Park Service, United States Forest Service, California State Park, and county, regional, and urban rangers and administrators. They felt that it was important for people to be able to survive in an environment that can be adverse, where sometimes a ranger's life, or that of a visitor, might depend upon the skill the ranger has to survive. I have been involved in several instances where that was so. Learning on the job is not an option. The class also taught people to respect what nature gave them in all conditions, as well as provided exercises in teamwork.

Attitude Adjustments

Mandated training not only took time away from regular duties to complete, but it also was a method to adjust or change attitudes. When you are programmed to do anything, you want to use what you learn. In fact, studies have been made that say that the more enforcement training you receive and equipment you get, the more enforcement incidents occur. You are more "tuned" to see things happen. You are anxious to use the new ways of doing things. It is an attitude adjustment! Sometimes park agencies have even paid to have their rangers go through some sensitivity training after attending enforcement academies to tone them down a little. Trained park rangers have a special enforcement demeanor, and they needed to be reprogrammed to use the lowest effective level before returning to the parks. Having an image that invites a ranger to be approachable is important, regardless of which agency you work for.

Being approachable is one of the major issues facing park law enforcement in today's environment. In the training I received, we were taught that people who find themselves in enforcement situations could be unpredictable and dangerous. Training causes rangers to be alert and to assume a defensive position in almost all situations. I have been told that the closer you are to training, the more unlikely you will get into trouble. It is the older, more experienced rangers who get assaulted, not those rangers right out of the academy. It is one of the reasons for enforcement training updates. To be approachable, rangers need to be able to recognize and handle those situations that are not threatening and not take a non-verbal defensive stance by habit. How to handle conflict verbally and recognizing the non-verbal communication signs are two of the most important skills any enforcement officer can have.

Also to be approachable you have to be visible and that might mean getting out of the patrol vehicle once in a while and "range." Rangers, after all, are public servants as well as enforcement officers. Recently a new park was designed in our county that put the ranger's offices in the maintenance yard instead of the visitor's center. The reasoning was so they would not be bothered by the park visitor.

Levels of Enforcement

I have always been taught that there was an enforcement "level" that you took into an enforcement issue. That standard is listed below in priority order from the least amount of force to the extreme. All require an important level of expertise and common sense on the part of the ranger:

1. **Education:** The violator, in the opinion of the ranger, can be educated and released. Being able to recognize that fact does take experience. Despite this being the lowest level, all enforcement contacts should have this educational level. Of course in some cases, like felonies, this might not be possible.

2. **Verbal warning and release:** Asking someone to stop what they are doing because ... Sometimes violators will even thank you afterwards.

3. **Written warning:** A written notice that your violation is on file with the agency's radio dispatcher. It can also be on file at park headquarters and referred to if a stop is made again. Repeaters usually allow the ranger to go to the next level.

4. **Citation:** A written notice of violation with a fine. Failure to pay becomes contempt of court. The thought here is that the probable cause of any violation that you have written has to hold up in court. This is also true in the next step, so much so that our magistrate had us write the probable cause of a citation on the back of copy of the written citation that went to court.

5. **Citation to Court:** Tell it to the judge. Let the judge decide the fine and disposition of the violator.

6. **Physical Arrest:** You are going to jail. Always cause a written incident report.

7. **Lethal force:** There have been some incidents in parks in this country where weapons were drawn and shots fired. There is a huge liability if you use a gun in a campground where there are tents and soft sided vehicles. This is very rare, however. I must agree that being armed gives a ranger a degree of comfort. I found that out when I went from being an armed ranger in the National Park Service to being an unarmed ranger in county parks.

You might notice as the list heads down toward the bottom, you get more into what police and sheriffs (as well as rangers in high visitation or more urban areas) usually do.

It could be that part of the rising crime statistics and higher levels of enforcement in parks are also a reflection of just who the supervisor is. The more emphasis the boss puts on what rangers do for enforcement, the more citations are written and the higher level used. More citations reflect on crime statistics. Sometimes those statistics also are used for budget purposes. The more incidents, the more people are required for enforcement. Not having the right numbers of rangers on duty because the agency cannot afford them is a bane to field-level rangers in every agency. Harry Batlin, a long time California state park ranger and administrator, used to say that when you give a citation to someone, it is also a citation about our failure to educate the people about how to behave in parks. He may be right! However, when someone sells cocaine to a park visitor, they should go straight to jail. There is no lowest level there.

When rangers who have spent a lot of time in the backcountry are put into a high enforcement situation, they might need an attitude adjustment to be hardened to the reality that bad people exist. I had that happen to me when I became a front country horse patrolman after being a backcountry ranger. I was put in Yosemite Valley for a month to have my attitude changed before I went to Tuolumne Meadows. I was first told that there was too much snow in Tuolumne for a horse, but later was told openly that I was there so I could make the transition to a law enforcement officer and to experience people who were not nice.

Changes at the Top

Changes over the years have occurred at the very top levels of park management in Washington, D.C., and in the case of California, in Sacramento. Over many years, the director of the National Park Service got there by moving up through the ranks. Always politically appointed by the President, directors were always National Park Service people. That changed during the Nixon Administration, when he fired George Hartzog and replaced him with Ron Walker, who had planned Nixon's trip to China. The same evolution has happened in Sacramento, where persons without park backgrounds have been appointed director.

It has been my observation over the years that the road to being the person in charge of parks in the National Park Service and in some state parks was always through the park ranger ranks. If you wanted to be a park superintendent in the National Park Service or a state park, or in any similar agency, then you had better have been a ranger. It was traditional. Trained law enforcement people are now occupying the decision-making seats in national parks and elsewhere. The generalist rangers are now retiring or have retired. In the past, those generalist rangers and a lot of maintenance people and interpreters were in the seats of administration that caused enforcement to take a back seat to other park issues. That policy sometimes placed protection rangers in danger by not supporting adequate training and not providing modern equipment. It is becoming a "Catch-22" situation. Supervisor positions are also being filled with people who have had no experience in (or formal introduction to) resource management or interpretation. They have no idea how important those fields are to management. Regional and county park departments sometimes have people with recreation majors or public administration degrees managing law enforcement. Unless that person can delegate well and trust the decisions that those people around them make, then those important divisions of parks could be in trouble.

An article by Megan Casserly told of the secret power of the generalist. Although the article targeted the business field, it had some close similarities to the park management world. The article stated that only by understanding the work within the fields to the right and left of your own can you understand the bigger picture, whether you are talking about a corporation or the world as a whole.[91]

Places like the Silicon Valley, which is full of specialists, actually are seeing a rise in generalists as supervisors. The article also says that when a society changes, the generalist is more flexible to that change. Casserly even used nature as an example. Some animals, like the koala, have great restrictions on how they live within their environment based upon an extremely limited set of conditions, yet other animals are very flexible to change. Some animals, like a mouse, can live in almost any environment and can survive almost anywhere.

Recently, a Little Hoover Commission report about the California state parks stated that state parks had management heavily represented by rangers with law enforcement training, that some of the stake-

---

[91] Megan Casserly, *"The Secret Power of the Generalist -- And How They'll Rule the Future,"* Forbes Woman, July 10, 2012.

holders (park visitors) have said contributes to a culture of law enforcement and protection, and has inhibited the department's ability to adapt quickly to change.[92] The Commission also stated that what the department needs is diversity in management: the agency should open its managerial ranks to professionals from outside the state and allow people without enforcement training to have managerial positions. Also suggested in the report is that California should address their ranger shortage by creating a "ranger generalist" classification and a separate classification for a "law enforcement ranger."[93]

Unionization

A ranger's job is never eight to five. The above words of wisdom were given to a group of backcountry rangers by Chief Ranger Bill Wendt during one of the summers when I worked in Yosemite. How correct Bill's words were. The nature of the job is that you are on duty on holidays and weekends, and there is coverage from opening to closing. In some parks that have camping, the park never closes. Many of the people that I questioned about why the profession was changing pointed to unionization. The new people who were coming into the profession didn't want to be paid in "sunsets," and rightfully so. Like all of us, they wanted a living wage, and they saw a union as the means for receiving it. Along with the negotiations that went with unions, however, there came very specific job descriptions and a "time element" for the job: eight hours a day, 40 hours a week. Certainly park employees do need to be treated fairly and kept safe, but adding fringe benefits and special enforcement equipment also causes strain on agencies financial resources.

The local rangers in the county where I live also negotiated the time to be spent on resource management and how many interpretive programs they had to give. By contract, working past the regular shift

---

[92] Little Hoover Commission Report, "Beyond Crisis: Recapturing Excellence in California's State Park System, Executive Summary" March 2013.
[93] Ibid.

time required overtime. "I only just work eight to five." Some old-timers just sadly shake their heads.

At one time, the negotiating unit within the California state parks was the California State Park Rangers Association (CSPRA). CSPRA included generalist rangers, interpreters, and ecologists, among others. When some California state park rangers felt threatened, there was a push to become armed and to attain peace officer status. After the decision to arm and train the rangers and offer POPE (Police Officer Protective Equipment), a new organization began. It would bring to the department a public safety union that became the new negotiating unit for the rangers and also brought a substantial raise in pay.[94] A few years ago, they successfully had their job titles changed to State Park Peace Officer/Ranger. CSPRA still exists, but is a mere shadow of what it used to be. Now I have been told by some retired state park rangers that the union is pretty much calling the shots in Sacramento.

In my 2013 survey, state park people and the local county and regional rangers mentioned unionization as a driving force that changed the job, but those with federal agencies did not. One California state park ranger told me that it became so bad, that maintenance people would become upset if rangers even picked up a piece of paper. The resource ecologists in California State Parks would not support projects like prescribed fire, "because that was their job." That attitude of specialization only left the law enforcement side of the job for the rangers to do.

Edward Abbey, noted outdoor author and former seasonal ranger, gives voice to this frustration in his book *Desert Solitaire*:

> Put the rangers to work. The lazy scheming loafers. They have wasted too many years selling tickets in toll booths and sitting behind desks filling out charts and tables in a vain effort to appease the mania for statistics which torments the Washington office. Put them to work. They're supposed to be rangers. Make the bums range! Kick them out of those over-

---

[94] Personal email from Harry Batlin, a former State Park Supervisor.

stuffed patrol cars and drive them out on to the trails where they should be, leading the dudes over hill and dale and safely into and back out of wilderness. It won't hurt them to work off a little office fat; it'll do them good...[95]

I used to give a talk to a class of graduating students in park management at West Valley College every year about the profession they were about to enter. A part of this talk has always been the reading of an entry in the daily log of park ranger John Wegner. Horace Albright found it in Yosemite in 1928. Mr. Albright, the second Director of the National Park Service, published this entry in his book *"Oh Ranger."* Across the top of this entry someone had written the words "All in a day's work." It is one of my favorite park stories and having been a ranger in Tuolumne at one time, I marvel at the endurance that Ranger Wegner possessed in this incident. I am not sure there are many rangers today who could have accomplished what he did. I know I probably could not. The distance to the top of Vernal Falls from Tuolumne Meadows is over 20 miles. From the falls to Yosemite Valley is another five or six miles and to El Portal, even more. I have ridden to Yosemite Valley from Tuolumne and it took me most of the day to get there. The entry went like this:

I got phone orders at Tuolumne Meadows to pack up and come in over Sunrise Trail.

Started at sunrise. Everything haywire, including a cranky pack horse which kept getting off the trail.

Phone in at the Vernal Falls station. Ordered to hurry down and help catch two car thieves who broke jail just after breakfast. Assigned the Culterville Road. Only transportation was the Chief's personal auto, which I could have if I could find the person who borrowed it from the Chief. Chief didn't know who that was.

Guarded the Culterville Road until 3 a.m. when ordered to the valley to beat the brush by the river with a flashlight to locate thieves. Found one thief and captured him just before dawn.

---

[95] Edward Abbey, *Desert Solitaire,* MacGraw Hill, 1968.

Somebody else assigned to guard him, but before I turned in I got orders to meet a carload of trout at El Portal and help plant them in some streams. Met fish OK, but coming up El Portal road, Quad truck slipped over the side of the road but was saved from going down the cliff by a tree. Cans of fish lashed to the truck so saved them. Job was complicated by necessity of keeping water aerated in cans sitting by the roadside while we rushed more water from small stream from one mile away. Fished all saved. Phoned for help, and kept water moving in the cans until the truck was dragged back on the road and fish cans reloaded.

Relieved of duty with nothing to do but walk nine miles and go to bed!

All in a day's work, indeed!

Chapter 12: Envisioning the Future of the Ranger Profession

A Ranger is "Everything to Everybody"

Some wise person out there once said that a "generalist is a person who knows a little bit about a lot, and keeps on learning less and less about more and more until they know nothing about everything." Also, the same person defined a "specialist" as a person who learns more and more about less and less, until they know everything about nothing. Alas, not so for a park ranger. Because lives can be saved or altered by the decisions of park rangers, their knowledge should be all encompassing. It is the park visitor's perception of what a ranger does. Learning just a little bit just doesn't do. I believe that to a park visitor, rangers are indeed, "everything to everybody."

When we talk of generalist rangers, what we are saying is that the ranger has a broader knowledge than a specialist, who has zeroed in on one thing. That "thing" is usually law enforcement. Even law enforcement rangers have first responder and search and rescue responsibility and in some agencies even can be certified to be a fire fighter.

Jack Morehead, a former Yosemite Superintendent, said, "Seasonal rangers (and all rangers, for that matter) were relied upon to represent the park, enforce park rules, perform law enforcement, respond to accidents, treat injuries, conduct searches, participate in technical rescues, protect the resources and values of the park, ensure visitors are safe during their visits, and explain the features of the area to visitors."[96] I could also add to Jack's description. You often find rangers relocating bears, giving interpretive talks, picking up after people, fixing trails, repairing leaking faucets, knowing where the good fishing is, plus doing a myriad of other things that are the "other duties as required" part of the job description. The generalist or traditional park ranger description also describes an approachable attitude that

---

[96] Thomas A. Smith, *"I'm Just a Seasonal,"* Productivity Productions, Rochester, New York, 2005.

visitors expect from a ranger. The description was not any different than if a ranger had been full time. Seasonal rangers thankfully did not have to put up with all the bureaucratic reports that the full-timers had to create.

Almost all rangers have personally cited people for violations that led to someone ending up in jail, rescued damsels in distress, searched for lost people, educated and given verbal warnings, gotten in "scary" law enforcement situations that required backup, helped relocate a bear or handled other wildlife problems, given impromptu interpretive talks, given formal living history presentations, helped pluck people off of rocks, ridden a horse miles and miles, packed a mule, and lived in sub-standard housing that not many people would have accepted, lacking electricity and hot water.

We also could, and usually did, tell people where to go to catch fish. There were some great places to fish in the park. However, I was often reluctant to tell people for selfish reasons. Another seasonal ranger I knew actually placed brush over a trailhead into a good fishing lake in the south end of the park so people could not find it. The brush was taken away eventually, and the trail was uncovered. The lake that had been artificially stocked by private packers (without permission) has now been fished out.

One of the questions I asked retired and active park rangers was why they wanted to be park rangers. Was it to spend their lives in a beautiful place like Yosemite? Was it their overwhelming love of things outdoors and natural? For almost everyone, it was all of those things. For me, Yosemite, Uvas Canyon, and Sanborn County Parks (Santa Clara County, California) were wonderful and interesting places to work. Certainly Yosemite was one of the crown jewels of the National Park System. Uvas Canyon, my first park, was then a small, 380-acre natural park in the foothills of the California Coast Range, with a campground of under 30 sites, a couple of picnic areas, and only a few miles of trails. It had its own system of waterfalls and cascading water, although, quite obviously, not even close to the height of Yosemite Falls or the beauty of Bunnell Cascades. Uvas was, in its own right, a beautiful little park in a wonderful county park system that belongs to the over one million citizens of Santa Clara County. Thanks to those citizens, Uvas Canyon is now over 2000 acres.

In some urban areas that do not have large natural parks in their systems, rangers do not get the diverse experiences that state and national park rangers do. When we asked former and present park rangers what drew them to the job, even those who had spent their entire careers in urban parks gave us similar answers. The reason most mentioned was an undying love for things natural and the great outdoors. It was always this love of the out-of-doors that ultimately got them into the profession.

> "I liked the idea of being a ranger naturalist, because I taught biology in high school."

> "It all began as a summer job when I was in college, and I ended up loving it."

> "I wanted a job in the outdoors where I could teach people about nature and show them how things worked and why."

> "My parents took me camping as a child and I learned to love the outdoors."

> "Being in Boy Scouts was a huge influence on me."

Scouting was also a big influence on me as a child. I became an Eagle Scout. I often worked with rangers, like NPS rangers Tom Habecker and Butch Farabee, who were also Eagle Scouts. There used to be no better place to get a land ethic than Scouting. The organization is now a lot different than when I went through it in the forties. It is more urbanized and selective as to membership.

There were two responses on my ranger survey that indicated that the person joined the ranger force because they liked the enforcement. Almost to a person, the results of my little survey showed that there was a passion and a commitment to protecting what they loved: the outdoors. The emphasis toward protecting people from other people was farther down on the priority list and was mentioned as "just part of what we do."

The Place for "Law Enforcement Specialists"

Is there room in this fast-paced society for a ranger that is everything to everybody? We believe so, although this question might never be answered. Each side of the issue has valid points to consider. I would want to encourage having the public safe when they are in parks and to make sure rangers are also protected. I also feel that through the years the job of the ranger really has never changed that much. Certainly enforcement training has changed what rangers emphasize. No matter what park or park agency, rangers have always had the responsibility to make sure park visitors have the feeling of safety. The ranger and the park also need to be safe, as well.

Jordon Fisher Smith, a California state park ranger, mentioned in his fine book, *"Nature Noir"* that even Galen Clark had the same problems in 1870 that we have today. Clark's first known arrest was someone cutting down a tree. There was also a report that Clark wrote that "crazy people on alcohol" liked to come to the mountains. As Smith said, "some things never change."[97]

Perhaps specialized enforcement officers are needed in some parks while not in others. Park enforcement is complex because it has become situational or site specific. It might make sense for rangers in high impact areas, like Lake Mead National Recreation Area, Yosemite Valley, California's beaches, or urban parks to be more enforcement oriented. That suggestion was made by the Little Hoover Commission that California look at two different types of rangers, state park police and ranger generalists. That does not excuse any ranger from using the lowest enforcement level and having the knowledge and ability, as well as the friendly and approachable attitude, to educate people on how to use their park.

There is also an issue of enforcement jurisdiction and the problem of being in isolated places. Who has the power to do what? Some national parks have exclusive federal jurisdiction. What that means is

---

[97] Jordon Fisher Smith, *"Nature Noir, A Park Ranger's Patrol in the Sierra,"* Houghton Miffon Company, New York, New York, 2005.

that the rangers are the enforcement because only federal law is applied. The parks were created on federal land. The California State Highway Patrol or local sheriff has no power inside the boundaries of Yosemite, as an example. As a result, Yosemite has a magistrate and a jail in Yosemite Valley. Not all national parks have that jurisdiction. Some of it is "shared" with the local sheriff. Most state park agencies are the same, as are local park agencies. Help by sheriff departments or local police can sometimes be pretty far away and that affects ranger safety. In California, designated state park rangers have state-wide authority like a fish and game warden and are not restricted to just state park property but can enforce county laws and even special open space district laws.

Protection rangers can point to dangers in which they are often placed. Border parks, like Organ Pipe National Monument, where Ranger Kris Eggle was shot and killed by a member of a Mexican drug cartel, are dangerous places. Enforcement at places like Organ Pipe is National Park Service enforcement. Rangers are certainly overmatched by people coming across the border. After this incident, officials of the Department of the Interior were blamed for downplaying crime in our parks in an effort to keep the "wholesome image."[98] Incidents like what happened to Ranger Eggle are rare. Each year there are over 400 million visits to the national parks, and add to that the millions that visit the national forests, Bureau of Land Management lands, and Bureau of Reclamation and Army Corps of Engineers reservoirs, state parks and regional, county and urban parks. I do believe that you are safer in a park than at home.

The drug cartels are also appearing in state and local parks and in places like Yosemite, and other government lands to grow marijuana. Of course this causes stressful situations for rangers. Yosemite and other national park units have had problems with pot growers. In the South San Francisco Bay Area, over a million dollars' worth of pot was taken from one county park and the state park across the road. It was not removed by rangers, however, but the Campaign Against Marijuana Growers (CAMP) a cooperative California organization

---

[98] ImmigrationHumanCost.org, "Law Loses Out at U.S. Parks"

that included law enforcement officers, game wardens, and other armed personnel. No manner of specialization is going to be successful if the money is not there to hire people to care for what needs to be done. Cutbacks in ranger staffing because of the lack of funding is a huge part of the reason for specialization. It leaves little time for the ranger to do anything else but keep visitors safe.

For several years in a row, Public Employees for Environmental Responsibility has noted that "law enforcement work" in the National Park Service is the most dangerous in the federal service. The Bureau of Labor Statistics has stated that the National Park Service suffers the worst record of having their officers killed or injured in the line of duty of any federal agency, even the FBI.[99] Certainly it was time for specialized training in enforcement.

In February 2007, a California State Parks Task Force (CRTF) studied whether the generalist model is still viable in the California State Park System. In the case of California, a "generalist" is one who patrols during the day and gives campfire talks at night, or gets involved in prescribed fire projects along with enforcement duties.

Hundreds of conversations took place among staff and task force members in a variety of subject matter. The CRTF looked at visitor attendance, staffing, both seasonal and full time, training, hiring practices, public safety issues, interpretive services, and the structure of other park agencies. The CRTF found that park enforcement and public safety has become more complicated and more time consuming. Funding shortages has caused a problem with operations.[100]

Resource management has decreased as a primary duty of rangers in light of increased specialization. However, the job was very different from one park to another. One California State Park Ranger I talked to recently actually plowed the snow off of the road during winter in his park. On a visit to a California off-road vehicle park, I actually saw a

---

[99] John T. Waterman, *The Demise of the Generalist Ranger*, an excerpt from *Ranger Magazine*, Summer 2008.
[100] Final report of the Generalist Ranger and Lifeguard Task Force, California State Parks, 2007.

ranger on a back hoe digging out a silt catch basin. The CRTF did admit that the California State Parks were to take into the account that the main goal is resource protection and the preservation of the traditional park culture. This means that everyone that is employed by State Parks is to support all aspects of the Department's mission. "Park culture" also means that a ranger is not only a figure of authority, but also a source of friendly information, but there has been a sense that rangers have decreased their approachability in recent years, most likely because of training in officer safety. It could be that during training rangers have been told that their vehicle is a source of protection for them, leading them to a reluctance to leave it to patrol areas on foot. Also the lack of staffing causes rangers to spend less time in one place while on patrol.

This task force also found that the wearing of the park Stetson hat was being challenged by the new people in the organization. The Stetson is a park ranger symbol. To the general public, it is a symbol that you are a ranger, the valuable park resource person who can rescue damsels in distress, take a drunk off the road, relocate a bear, identify a tree, and tell people where the good fishing is. California State Parks has found that the rangers have taken an aversion to wearing that symbol, and suggests that new employees start wearing it more often when in training in "order to get used to it." County park rangers in California only wear the Stetson in formal Class A uniform situations. In Yosemite, we wore it all the time. Even in the backcountry.

I find it interesting that other enforcement agencies have started wearing the same ranger Stetson. Why? Because of the image it has that the wearer is someone you can approach. They got that from parks. When I first worked in county parks, the hat was a cowboy type hat, like that worn by the USFS. Rangers were successful in having that replaced by the traditional ranger Stetson. Why? One of the reasons was that in a dark campground a visitor could know immediately who you were just by the hat you were wearing. The other reason was that it was a symbol of someone who was approachable. The California State Park Rangers and the Association of National Park Rangers have the Ranger Stetson as a symbol of their organization.

Working in a campground is not like working a city street because the campground is filled with tents and soft-sided vehicles. Highways may be different, but few rangers have that responsibility unless you are in a large national park somewhere where jurisdiction is exclusive. However California state park rangers can pull over a speeding motorist on a state highway if they encounter one when traveling from one park to another.

Of course, there is a huge responsibility when carrying a firearm. In my 15 years in Yosemite, I never had to pull my weapon out of the holster in an enforcement situation.

I admit that wearing the weapon gives you a feeling of security you wouldn't have if you were not armed. It could also be a determent to the criminals. In our local county park system, I often felt uncomfortable when making a law enforcement contact without the armed protection that I was used to having in NPS.

The National Park Service Social Science Program supported by the Institute for Conservation Law Enforcement conducted a literature review for Shenandoah National Park. They found that research on personal values, motivators, and behaviors of NPS law enforcement work was very limited. Information on visitor perceptions is also limited. Most research dealt with crime rates and focused more on the working environment than on the rangers themselves.[101] Research on the effectiveness of the mission is non-existent, which is somewhat surprising because of the long debate that has been taking place over the proper roles of the park ranger. That research would be helpful in dealing with the "new society" of visitors.

The "Ideal Ranger"

If we had the power to construct or to hire the "ideal ranger," what would that person look like? The interpretive supervisor in the Santa Clara County park agency, Robin Schaut, told me that she would like to see "a ranger that would get on their knees to show a flower to a

---

[101] National Park Service Social Science Program Literature Review.

child." There is a lot to say about that statement. You can still be a law enforcement specialist and do that. Most park administrators feel the ideal ranger would be an approachable person who has the knowledge and the patience and demeanor to educate and use the lowest level of enforcement. It should be a ranger able to recognize and successfully head toward the other end of the enforcement spectrum when needed. It should be a person with a level head in stressful situations and a professional demeanor.

Lisa Killough, former Director of Santa Clara County Parks, hit the nail right on the head in an email to me in September, 2013. She said that "ranger law enforcement is a critical part of the job of a park ranger and should be performed to the spirit not the letter where education of the park customer is essential. She added that rangers should help people help themselves, whether it is in the area of education, stewardship, or public safety. Every good ranger is part public safety officer, part counselor, part teacher, and part savior (hero). Rangers need to know their parks and embrace the natural environment and the joy of sharing this knowledge with others."

I believe that it is important that a ranger be physically fit to do the job. Someone's life may depend upon it, including that of the ranger's. The National Park Service, California State Parks, and one of our local open space agencies have fitness standards and give their field level people time off during their duty day to keep fit. When I worked in Yosemite, we could take 30 minutes from my duty hours to work on my fitness. I am certain that there are many agencies throughout the United States that have that requirement, as well. I know of an agency that tried to have a fitness standard and was denied by the union because they could not prove that fitness was a part of the job.

Most protection for the visitor comes through enforcement presence. Ranger visibility is essential. A well-patrolled park has the least crime and vandalism. I always thought that just being visible made the horse such a valuable tool in enforcement. The horse was watching where he was going and you were watching what was going on! Just sitting in a turnout in a patrol vehicle along a park road slowed vehicles down. Rangers do need to exit their vehicles once in a while and walk through campgrounds and places where people congregate. Of course a well-funded park system has enough rangers on duty so that can happen.

If we are to save parks for future generations, then the rangers have to become the heroes like the traditional rangers of the past. Lee Shackleton said, "It is the essence of the National Park Service that distinguishes it from other agencies. That being a ranger is a matter of spirit. It is a spirit that grows during a person's career. Rangers must possess a deep and genuine personal feeling for the American concept of the perpetuation of our highest scenic, historic, and natural areas in such a way to ensure their integrity for the enjoyment of future generations."[102]

Mandated training must again include the broader spectrum about what the job is all about. The rangers should be introduced to the culture of parks and the historical evolution of how the profession came about. There is nothing wrong with including mandated training in methods to protect resources and provide interpretation. Rangers must again become pure and simple. Knowledge about the park they work in and attitudes, we fear, are the only differences between being a generalist or traditionalist and strictly a park enforcement officer.

What will the crystal ball tell us about park rangers? What will they look like in the future? Right at this moment, the old-time generalist attitudes look to be a thing of the past. Park rangers in other agencies are crying for more specialization, not less. Rangers seem to be fading away from the attitudes that presented a "park face" to visitors. I hope that in this document, I have made a case for using the lowest effective enforcement level. We need to at least bring back the "spirit" mentioned by Lee Shackleton.

The Crystal Ball

Former National Park Service Ranger Tom Habecker shared with me an incident that happened when he was coming out of a park build-

---

[102] Lee Shackleton, personal email communication, July 6, 2006.

ing in a large crowd of people. A little boy, perhaps five years old, upon seeing Tom, stopped in his tracks, stood at attention and saluted, saying "Hello sir." Tom stopped, saluted back, and said "Hi." Tom said that when he was leaving the building, he had a lot on his mind, but that kid saw him as a hero, an image. It made Tom's day, and he has never forgotten it. Yes, he was wearing the "flat hat" and not some baseball cap. Every once in a while we just have to be reminded as to who we are and what we represent.[103]

I was talking to a California state park ranger one day about an article I had read, and he told me that he wished he had the time to read. I told him it was his job to take the time to read. It was a ranger's professional duty to at least try to keep ahead of the new ideas and science that is appearing in their profession. After a long pause, he agreed with me.

Rangers need to be avid readers about the environment, particularly as it pertains to park issues. It should be a part of the job of every park management teacher and park administrator to be informed and up to date on issues like what we are facing today — not particularly to change views, but to make students and staff do more critical thinking where critical thinking is needed. I have a recommended reading list at the end of this book. The books mentioned are those from my personal library.

I once wrote a column in the *Signpost*, a newsletter from PRAC (Park Rangers Association of California) about new books on parks and related park management. I did this hoping to tweak an interest in reading. I do know some who were inspired to read, but most often people in the profession were not. That is alarming. Other than up-to-date training and professional conferences that a lot of agencies have little funding for, the only other way for rangers to get information to make their life easier is to read. Right now, professional ranger organizations like CSPRA and PRAC are in membership trouble. An organization's annual conferences are a place to learn and to exchange ideas, but rangers are not up to spending their own money to attend.

---

[103] Tim Habecker, personal communication.

Those who do spend their own money are seemingly the devoted ones.

How do you become a hero? You can become one in the eyes of visitors and your fellow rangers by just trying to be the best and the most professional that you can be. Rangers who strive to be the best are the ones who are the most successful. That works in sports as well as it does in any profession. Maybe, like Tom Habecker, you can propagate your own heroes by being just who you are.

I have become concerned that there is presently no one like Mather or Albright or Mott, to advocate for the parks.

Many modern-day people, like Alfred Runte, have certainly made an impact upon parks through what they have written. What I would like is for someone to step up and pound on the podium until someone listens to the fact that parks and the natural spaces everywhere in America are in trouble. Lovers of the environment like to discuss these issues by using the phrase; "the canary in the coal mine." Parks and the protection they provide are the "canaries" for things natural. As we have seen, most adverse things that happen to parks come from outside the boundaries.

I would like to pass on to you that, in my opinion, the fact that most people who are coming into the ranger profession are without passion and knowledge of the outdoors, is one of the "canaries" for outdoor spaces almost everywhere. Park rangers need to become heroes again to young people by making education about the outdoors a huge priority, not just a passing fancy or an afterthought.

Santa Clara County has a weeklong outdoor education program for fifth graders. Maybe those young people need to meet and greet a park ranger during that session who can tell them what parks are all about. It is time to educate the future park visitors and maybe inspire the future park rangers.

In an editorial in their newsletter, CNANP President Maureen Finnerty stated that the Coalition was making great progress to hopefully establish a "Park Stewardship Institute," which will elevate the national conversation on the value of parks in and of themselves and their contributions to our quality of life. They are looking for opportunities to spread the good news about parks.[104]

Every park agency employee should stand up to that challenge, especially "on the ground" people like rangers, interpreters, maintenance people, people at visitor center desks, and wilderness permit issuers. We need to turn again to those kinds of people who do the job of managing parks and all it entails with a passion and not treat it as "just a job." Passion is a big word when it comes to being a ranger and what rangers represent.

Doug Morris stated in his conclusion of the ranger renewal document he wrote for the Coalition to Protect America's National Parks that "there is clearly an emotional bond between the people of this country and its parks. There is, as well, a deep affection for those men and women who protect park resources, provide a safe and enjoyable park experience, and inspire understanding of park values. The park ranger in the now-familiar 'flat hat' long ago became the human image of our national parks and other park systems around the world. It is clearly time, once again, to assume the burden of leadership in a comprehensive effort to renew the park ranger profession."[105] All state, regional and local park agencies also need to meet that challenge.

---

[104] CNPSR 10th Anniversary Newsletter, November 2013.
[105] Morris, op. cit.

Appendix A - Recommended Reading for Park Lovers

People seriously interested in parks might turn to author Roderick Nash, Professor Emeritus of Environmental Science at University of California, Santa Barbara, and author of *Wilderness and the American Mind* and *The Rights of Nature*. Or they might like to read books written by Michael Frome, who has written many critical books and articles about the National Parks and the outdoors, like the *"Re-greening of the National Parks."* Albert Runte and David Brower are excellent and prolific authors that I highly recommend. David was the former President of the Sierra Club and the founder of Friends of the Earth. Runte is one of the premier outdoor writers in America and a former seasonal interpreter in Yosemite.

As I used to tell my students at West Valley College, resource books cost money, but they are worth it when you might glean an idea that makes your job easier and more effective. Can you place a price on an idea that works?

I have many notebooks of lecture notes and hard files that I also turned to when writing this document. At my age, I am trying to get rid of things. My national park library went to Cal Poly San Luis Obispo. I had over 70 books in my library just on the National Park Service. Obviously, those cannot be listed below. I am the "ultimate parkie" and a lover of books. Put those two loves together and you have a room full of resources. What are listed are books that are still on my shelves and which I used to supplement my professional expertise as I wrote this book.

Being a Ranger and Ranger History

Albright, Horace, *Creating the National Park Service, The Missing Years*, University of Oklahoma Press, Norman, Oklahoma, 1999. With the help of daughter Marian Albright Schenck, this book tells about the early years in the struggle to create the National Park Service. A must read for historian interested in this era.

Bingaman, John W., *Guardians of the Yosemite,* End-Kian Publishing Company. Lodi, California. First printing 1961. One of the first Yosemite Rangers, John tells about his career in the Park from 1918 until 1956. This book is still on sale in the Yosemite Visitor Centers and tells about how rangers evolved in Yosemite. Anyone interested in learning the early history of rangers should read this document. I have had a copy for many years and it is threadbare from use.

Brown, Richard E. (Rick), *Ranger Up,* Author House, Bloomington, Indiana, 2010. As I read Rick's book, it was interesting to me that his job in mostly eastern national parks was very similar to mine in Yosemite, except I was a seasonal employee and never became a supervisor. In Yosemite we had rock rescues, car clouting, crime against resources, water rescues, just like he experienced only in a different environment. Rick tells why and how to be the typical ranger. He gives vivid descriptions of incidents and educates the park visitor as to what they can do to protect themselves while visiting a national park. This interesting book in some cases seemed like reading an incident report.

Burnett, James, *Hey Ranger,* Taylor Trade Publishing, Boulder, Colorado, 2005. True tales of humor and misadventure from America's national parks. This document has stories that Ranger Burnett accumulated during his career in NPS.

Bytmar, Bruce W. *A Park Ranger's Life, Thirty Two Years Protecting Our National Parks,* Wheatmark, Tucson, Arizona, 2012. This is an interesting book about a modern NPS ranger in the jurisdictional nightmare that is Blue Ridge Parkway, North Carolina. By Ranger Bytmar's admission, he has been a commissioned law enforcement officer, structural and wildland firefighter, natural resource and historical interpreter, search and rescue manager, public health inspector, incident commander, park planner, supervisor, and manager. Most of his experiences were on the Blue Ridge Parkway, a 467-mile linear highway that connects the Shenendoah and Great Smokies National Parks. Ranger Bytmar not only was a ranger, but a highway patrolman and sheriff all in one. Bytmar does not pull any punches when he recalls working with no budget and little help.

Chavez, Carl S., *A Pathway through Parks*, CZ Publications Graeagle, California. A book about Carl's 33-year career in California State Parks which ended in 1998, it includes what it was like to raise a family and to work as a state park ranger and supervisor, and the effects of moving from park to park in the State of California.

Engbeck, Joseph, H. Jr., *State Parks of California*, Graphic Arts Center, Portland, Oregon, 1980. This is an excellent and well-illustrated book on the evolution and development of a state park system.

Everhart, William, *Take Down Flag and Feed the Horses*, University of Illinois Press, 1998. This is a document about the career of a permanent national park ranger mostly in Yellowstone National Park.

Farabee, Charles R. Jr, *The National Park Ranger, An American Icon*, Roberts Rinehart Publishers, Lanham, Maryland, 2003. This book is the "bible" for the evolution of the park ranger in the National Park Service. One of those people that I consider to be a ranger's ranger, "Butch" has written several other books about being a ranger and dealing with searches, rescues, and death in parks.

Hampton, H. Duane, *How the U.S Cavalry Saved Our National Parks*, University of Indiana Press, Bloomington, Indiana, 1972. This book is an excellent history in the protection of Yellowstone and Yosemite. I believe that the cavalryman were really our first "rangers" in the history of the profession. The only difference was they were not called rangers. Many of these early people did leave the army to become members of the new National Park Service. You might find it hard to find. When I ordered it lately, there were only a few known to be available.

Lankford, Andrea, *Ranger Confidential, Living, Working, and Dying in the National Parks*. (Copyright, Andrea Lankford 2010.) This is an interesting book about the life of a woman ranger in Yosemite. It discusses what it was like to be a woman in a "man's world," and how frustrating that was. An eye opener for me, but a good read.

Lynch, Michael G. *Images of America, California State Park Rangers*, (Arcadia Publishing Company, San Francisco, California 2009.) Mike is a 35 year veteran of California State Parks and a noted historian. This book is one in the pictorial series on Images of America by Arcadia. It traces, through pictures, the history of California's State Park Rangers.

Lynch, Michael G. *Rangers of California State Parks,* (Copyright by the author, 1996.) Mike's book is a nicely illustrated and excellent document on the history of the State Park Ranger in California.

Marty, Sid, *Men for the Mountains,* (McClelland and Steward Ltd, Toronto Canada, 1978 and republished by Emblem, 2008) Sid Marty wrote this when he was a Warden for Parks Canada. It is one of my favorite books about being a ranger because Sid had experiences like I had in Yosemite. He was a seasonal backcountry ranger, became full-time, and was shuffled off to the front country in Banff, one of Canada's most visited parks. Of course, I never became full-time. I read this book many years ago when I was a ranger in Yosemite, loaned it to someone, and never got it back. The book took a while to arrive because it comes from out of the country. My Amazon order took three weeks. Sid's book makes me glad that Yosemite did not have Grizzly bears to contend with, and at the same time, sad that they were no longer there. He went through not being able to get away with family because of events always seemed to happen on his days off. That happened to me several times when I worked in Tuolumne. Sid writes with great humor. A delightful read.

McLane, Dennis, *Seldom Was Heard an Encouraging Word, A History of Bureau of Land Management Law Enforcement,* (Shoppe Foreman Publishing, Guthrie Oklahoma, Copyright 2011.) McLane is the retired Chief of Bureau of Land management (BLM) Law Enforcement and also had a short career in both regional parks (Sacramento County California) and the California State Park and Recreation Department. This book is a complete history of how law enforcement evolved in the BLM from its beginnings in the Federal General Land Office and the Grazing Service and how the agency struggled to enforce the early land laws in this country. An interesting read.

Moody, Warren, *Yosemite Ranger on Horseback,* (Pioneer Publishing Company, Fresno, California, 1990.) This book is an interesting description of what a backcountry ranger did in Yosemite in the late

1920s, compared to what backcountry ranger did in the 1970s. The jobs were almost virtually the same.

Moomaw, Jack C. *Reflections of a Rocky Mountain Ranger,* (Revised Edition), (Copyright 1994 YMCA of the Rockies, Estes Park Colorado.) Jack grew up in the Rockies and guided "dudes" in Rocky Mountain National Park until a supervisor liked what he saw, and offered him a job. The year was 1922. Jack spent his whole career in Rocky. He was a poet, and the book is sprinkled with his poetry.

Myer, John Michael, *Ranger Stories, True Stories Behind the Ranger Image,* (Cold Tree Press, Nashville, Tennessee, 2005.) This book is written by a ranger who had a career in both the National Park Service and the Bureau of Land Management. It consists of a series of incidents that Myer went through while on duty with these two agencies as he "bounced around" the country as you often have to do to get ahead. It brings out some of the dangers of operating as a park ranger on the border of this country with Mexico.

Sargent, Shirley, *Protecting Paradise, Yosemite Rangers 1898-1960* (Ponderosa Press, Yosemite, California, 1998.) My cherished autographed copy is in a place of prominence on my book self. Shirley was a Yosemite icon, published 11 books on Yosemite, and edited several more. She offered to read my draft of my book on seasonals in Yosemite and offered only one suggestion: "The chapters are too short!" Shirley passed away a few years ago and will be sorely missed.

Schullery, Paul, *Mountain Time, a Yellowstone Memoir,* (Reprinted from a 1984 edition Nick Lyons/Schocken 2008.) Paul is a former Yellowstone Naturalist in the early '70s who was called back to work in the park as a writer. The book is a great document about the natural history of the Yellowstone region, told as only a former NPS interpreter could do. At the back of his book is an excellent list of Yellowstone resource books.

Sholly, Dan, Newman, Steven M. *Guardians of Yellowstone: An Intimate Look at the Challenges of Protecting America's Foremost Wilderness Park,* (Quill, 1993.) This book is a modern version of what a National Park ranger does. Dan was the chief ranger at the time of the Yellowstone fires and covers the politics of that event in detail as well as what it is like to be a national park ranger.

Smith, Jordan Fisher, *Nature Noir, A Ranger's Patrol of the Sierra*, (Houghton Mifflin Company, Boston, New York, 2005.) Jordon patrolled the American River Canyon for the California State Parks for 14 years. An interesting and often humorous depiction of what a park ranger does in the California State Park System.

Smith. Thomas A., *I'm Just a Seasonal*, (Productivity Productions, Rochester, New York, 2005.) This is my book on being a ranger in the '70s and '80s in Yosemite when most seasonal people were either teachers or students. It also illustrates some of the differences between backcountry and front country duty.

Van Cleve, David H, *Have a Nice Day, Job*, (Published by the Author, and printed in San Bernadino, California 2013.) Van Cleve was a California State Park Ranger, an ecologist and a park superintendent. This book is a humorous description of his career from beginning to end.

Park and Resource Management

Callicott, J.Baird, *In Defense of a Land Ethic, Essays in Environmental Philosophy*, (State University of New York Press, 1989.) The one part of this book that I really enjoyed was the section that dug deeply into the philosophy of Aldo Leopold. Other parts of the volume were kind of deep.

Carle, David, *Introduction to Fire in California*, (University of California Press, Berkeley, California, 2008.) This book, part of a series of books about California natural history, is wonderfully done by a former California state park ranger and introduces the reader to how fire affects the environment. This is a great book for people who are volunteer docents as well as for professional park people, including rangers.

Frome, Michael, *Regreening the National Parks* (The University of Arizona Press, Tucson, Arizona, 1992.) In an interesting and sometimes critical style, Frome covers everything in this book, from resource management to the demise of who he calls "Ranger Rick."

Goudie, Andrew, *The Human Impact on the Natural Environment*, (5th edition, MIT Press, Cambridge Massachusetts, 2000.) This book is a textbook that I used as a resource when I team taught a hospitality class at San Jose State University in 2000 on sustainable recreation. It covers many of man's impacts on vegetation, wildlife, soil, water, and the climate. It reads like a text book, but contains some very interesting things for a resource manager.

Howe, Jim, McMahon, Ed, Probst, Luther, *Balancing Nature and Commerce in Gateway Communities*, (Island Press, 1990.) A great book on how parks affect commerce in gateway communities, and vice versa.

Knight, Richard, and Landres, Peter, B., *Stewardship Across Boundaries*, (Island Press, Covelo, California, 1998.) The book is edited by Knight and Landres. It is the only book I know of that deals with the problems we are facing in some park agencies today and fostering partnerships and other administrative actions that one can take. In our area the biggest problem is encroachment by development. It talks of all kinds of boundaries, including some case studies. If one is not familiar with Island Press, it is the only nonprofit publisher of books on the environment in the United States.

Lowery, William R. *Repairing Paradise, The Restoration of Nature in America's National Parks*, (Brookings Institution Press, Washington, D.C. 2009.) In interesting book about the trials and tribulations of conducting several resource management projects, including wolves in Yellowstone, auto impacts in Yosemite, Everglades water problems, and the river flow in Grand Canyon. Also includes a chapter on changing policies in NPS and how to repair the damage from past policies. Not too technical and an interesting read.

Machlis, Gary E., Field, Donald R., *National Parks and Rural Development*, (Island Press, Covelo, California, 2000.) This book talks about the mistakes made and the successes of some national parks in dealing with encroachment by development. There are several supporting case studies included in the document.

MacKinnon, J.B. *The Once and Future World*, (Houghton Mifflin Harcourt Boston, New York, 2013.) I was browsing our local book store after Christmas in 2013, and as always made a trip by their "nature" section. I do not know what made me reach for this book, but I did and was very glad of it. Like Louv, Mackinnon emphasizes people reaching out to nature and becoming tuned to it again. He calls the attempt "wilding America." Along the way, he makes a stab at describing what "natural" means and touches on the dilemma of park managers in meeting their resource management missions based upon restoring to natural conditions, a task, he suggests, is almost impossible.

O'Brien, Bob R, *Our National Parks and the Search for Sustainability,"* (University of Texas Press, 1999.) The book explores the attempts by some national parks to balance use with nature. It includes some interesting case studies.

Runte, Alfred, *Yosemite, The Embattled Wilderness,* (University of Nebraska Press,1990.) Runte, who is considered a leading authority on park and park management has authored another book; the *National Parks, As American Experience.* This book was also published by Nebraska Press. *Embattled Wilderness* is just not another of those books about Yosemite. It is a book that looks at the aesthetic values of the park and at the management of Yosemite's resources, particularly wildlife. Runte was also an interpretive ranger in Yosemite at one time in his career.

General Interest

Beverage, Charles, E, Larkin, David, *Frederick Law Olmsted, Designing the American Landscape,* (Rizzoli International Publications, New York, New York, 1995.) Almost a coffee table book, this is the best that I have found on the life of Olmsted, who some call the father of the American park idea. The book is filled with beautiful photographs taken by Paul Rocheleau of Olmsted designed parks and other places in this country that Olmsted touched. Rocheleau is a senior photographer for several magazines, and has published several books. This book was edited and designed by David Larkin.

Brinkley, Douglas, *The Quiet World, Saving Alaska's Wilderness Kingdom,*(HarperCollins Books, New York, 2011.) Brinkley also wrote an excellent book on Teddy Roosevelt and his devotion to conservation entitled *"Wilderness Warrior."*

Quiet World is about how the Alaska wilderness was saved and those who were instrumental on getting that done. Brinkley is a wonderful writer and I had a difficult time putting this book down.

Louv, Richard, *Last Child in the Woods,* (Algonquin Books. 2008. Like Rachel Carson's *"Silent Spring,"* which pointed out how pesticide use was affecting our environment, Louv's book is a wake-up call to all of us who passively stand by while our children forget about the environment around them. Louv calls the lack of any feeling for the outdoors "nature deficit disorder," points out that far too many of our youth have that condition and warns of the danger that is going to bring in the future.

Louv, Richard, *The Nature Principle,* (Algonquin Books, 2011.) This second of Louv's masterpieces brings forth an idea that lands are available where people live, not only "out there' in the boonies" and that people should take advantage of their presence. Also looks at the adult side of "nature deficit disorder."

Appendix B - Park Ranger Survey

The following are the results of a survey that I passed out at the Annual California Park Conference in Seaside California in March, 2013. The Conference is attended by members of the California State Park Rangers Association (CSPRA) and the Park Rangers Association of California (PRAC). I also sent the same survey via email to 22 members of our local county park system. Total surveys in the hands of people numbered 52. It is a very small sampling to be a valid survey. My comments are in parentheses. A summary of the ranger's comments are at the end of the survey.

1. What agency do you work for?
   a. Federal: 2
   b. State: 7
   c. Regional or County: 28
   d. Municipal: 3
   e. Water District or other land management agency: 2
      (*Not surprising in that most of the attendees of the Conference were from PRAC.*)

2. What position do you hold?
   a. Park Ranger/Protection: 7
   b. Park Ranger/Generalist: 21
   c. Resource Management Technician
   d. Interpretive naturalist: 1
   e. Other:
      Supervisor: 1
      Caretaker: 1
      (*See above*)

3. What made you become a park ranger?
   a. Love working in the outdoors: 14
   b. Like the enforcement aspects of the job: 4

c. Wanted to educate people about how to take care of the environment: 11
d. Wanted to manage and maintain natural resources: 9
e. All of the above: 15

(These responses were similar to my first survey of mostly re-tired rangers except four out of the six protection rangers said they became rangers because of the enforcement part of their job. Most rangers I knew disliked the enforcement part of their jobs.)

4. What do you feel is the most important aspect of your job? Please place a number in front of each answer below in priority order. *(Scale of 1-5 with 1 being most important)*

a. Protecting people from other people (Enforcement): 2.9
b. Protecting the people from themselves (Search and rescue and education): 2.5
c. Protecting the people from the park (Facility safety and search and rescue): 2.2
d. Protecting the park from the people (Resource management and interpretation): 2.0
e. Other (Please describe) All equal 1

(I am surprised by this result. If two people are fighting in the campground and you got a report that another person was carving his initials in a tree, which incident has the priority? Certainly protecting the park is the real reasons for rangers, but protecting people is the number one priority and a moral issue.)

5. Do you feel that there is a changing culture among park rangers toward a more specialist role?
a. Yes: 21
b. No: 10

(Not surprising. It is the trend.)

6. If you answered yes to 5, do you feel that unionization of the profession had anything to do with the changing culture?
a. Yes: 5

b. No: 8

c. No opinion: 6

(*One response came to me from an Oklahoma State Park where there is no union representing the rangers, but that is moving toward unionization. Funding has caused the ranger staff at this individual's park agency to go from 100 in 1990 to a little above 40 now. Of course, less staff, more specialization, and rangers are being staffed at the parks with more incidents.*)

7. Have you seen a rising crime rate in your park agency?
   a. Yes: 18
   b. No: 10
   c. Do not know: 1

8. If your answer is yes to the above, circle the appropriate answer below
   a. Felonies: 1
   b. Misdemeanors: 6
   c. Local ordinances: 3
   d. All of the above: 9

9. What do you see as the most important item about the future of the park ranger and your parks? Please rank in priority order.
   a. Encroachment of parks by development: 4.2
   b. Overuse of parks causing damage to resources: 2.9
   c. More enforcement specialization: 3.8
   d. Funding for training: 2.8
   e. Enforcement training
   f. Interpretive training
   g. Resource management training
   h. Lack of a land ethic by visitors. "Nature Deficit Disorder.": 4.6
   i. Lack of park funding: 2.0

j. Other

(I was really interested in this part of the survey. The fact that the lack of park funding was the one that they choose the most was not a surprise. I was somewhat surprised by the reaction to the two questions about encroachment and land ethic. Either the rangers are not seeing encroachment as a threat, or it is too early for them to see the problem. It is a huge problem in the county where I live and in some national and state parks. Land ethic answer was also a surprise. That is one of the issues facing rangers in the near future. Enforcement specialization was also rated lower than I thought. We certainly are headed that way, but the rangers do not see that as a problem.)

10. Has your job changed over the years to a more specialist role?
    a. Yes: 6
    b. No: 11

Ranger Survey Comments

Maybe crime rates are connected to the poor economy or just more people?

I am a generalist and enjoy all facets of the job, but crime is rising.

Conflict in my agency between customer service and enforcement. Many rangers are interested in more enforcement and become disappointed in limitations brought on by management and that causes a high turnover rate.

My career has changed but not by choice.

Armed or not, some of the younger rangers group seem unclear on the meaning of the lowest level of enforcement.

With reduced staff we have less time to work on visitor services, protecting resources, etc. The time is not by choice but rather by need. If you only have three rangers in a district, it is hard to conduct a junior ranger program

An obvious bias survey. When is this issue going to stop? We are all trained to where we work. The only factor to specialization is lack of staff. In twenty years we have gone from 5 rangers to 1/3 of that spread over 3 counties in the Santa Cruz Mountains.

I have specialized in some aspects but I still clean restrooms, pick up trash, build trails, electrical and plumbing and general carpentry, resource management and still have time to interpret the park. True generalist!

Park agencies need to break the barriers of the park boundaries and join forces to work together. *(I assume with neighbors.)* Need now more than ever.

Important is the political will in defining the scope of duties. The more narrow the scope with law enforcement hampers the ability of the park ranger to maintain their safety and the safety of the visitor,

Enforcement is the number one priority with protective equipment, even though I never thought I would say that. Pot farm, guns, drugs are a part of the current trends and you do not know when you will come face to face with them.

Management. "Do as I say, not as I do" is a problem.

The following is the result of a 1979 survey that was sent to every agency in California (Except federal agencies) that had park rangers on their staff to ascertain that, if an academy was established to train rangers in law enforcement, what subjects/hours would they think would necessary for their rangers to have in their training. The survey listed all subjects and the training hours for full POST certified training for police officers that, at the time, was 400 hours. As stated in the introduction of the book, the results were presented to POST by the author with little results. The required training by most agencies was Penal Code 832, the laws of Arrest, Search and Seizure (40 hours) and the * items are included in 832. There was some movement by POST after the author presented the results to POST and they upped the hours to 60. (with firearms) An unusual fact was that we received

100% response. As of this writing 832 (2014) is still only 40 hours and 64 hours with firearms.

West Valley College Ranger Law Enforcement Training Program

Professional Orientation (7 hours)
Ethics and Professionalism (The Ranger Image)*: 2
The criminal justice system: 5

Human Relations (24 hours)
Public Relations (The Ranger Image): 2
Race and ethnic relations : 4
Interpersonal communications : 12
Stress and conflict management: 4
Crisis management : 2

Law (30 hours)
Constitutional law and civil liberties : 6
Criminal Law (Penal Code): 6
Laws of detention and arrest *: 8
Juvenile law and procedures: 10

Laws of Evidence (15 hours)
Evidence: 7
Search and seizure *: 8

Written communications
Report writing : 8

Vehicle operations (4)
Code three driving and operations: 4

Force and weaponry (7)
Moral and legal aspects: 3
Chemical agents: 4

Patrol Procedures (47)
Patrol and observation: 8
Vehicle stops: 2
Using the radio: 2

Searching and handcuffing techniques: 4
Crimes in progress: 4
Intoxication and disorderly conduct: 2
Domestic/civil: 1
Narcotics and dangerous drugs: 6
Abnormal behavior: 2
Crowd control : 3
Fish and game code : 1
News media relations-discretionary decision making : 8
Disaster training : 2

Traffic (12)
Vehicle code : 2
Drunk driving: 2
Citations : 2
Traffic control : 2 | Off-road vehicles: 2
Accident investigation : 2

Criminal Investigation (10)
Preliminary investigation : 2
Crime scene recording : 2
Collection and preservation of evidence: 4
Courtroom demeanor : 2

Defensive tactics and physical fitness (15)
Defensive tactics : 15

Visitor safety (4)
Liability : 2
Law suits and tort claims : 2

Examinations and tests (10)
Written and performance :10

Total hours: 193

*P.C. 832

Index

About the Author

Thomas A. Smith is a retired coordinator and instructor in park management from West Valley College in Saratoga, California, and had over 20 years of experience as a seasonal park ranger with the National Park Service and the Santa Clara County Department of Parks and Recreation. In 1986, the County borrowed him from the College to act as an interim director/full-time consultant for the park system while they conducted a nationwide search for a new director. He served as the Director of the Region Five Recreation Academy for the United States Forest Service held at West Valley College for 11 years until retirement. He started and served as director of a highly successful in-service training program for park rangers at West Valley that served agencies throughout the West Coast.

He received the first honorary lifetime membership to the Park Rangers Association of California (PRAC), and is one of the founding fathers of the organization. In 2012, he received the President's Award from the California Association of Park and Recreation Boards and Commissioners for his contributions to parks and recreation in California.

CPSIA information can be obtained
at www.ICGtesting.com
Printed in the USA
LVOW02s0523160117
521061LV00004B/12/P

9 781611 702026